Learning Construct 2

Design and create your own engaging, extensible, and addictive game using Construct 2

Aryadi Subagio

BIRMINGHAM - MUMBAI

Learning Construct 2

First published: December 2014

Production reference: 1201214

Published by Packt Publishing Ltd.
Livery Place
35 Livery Street
Birmingham B3 2PB, UK.

ISBN 978-1-78439-767-8

www.packtpub.com

Credits

Author
Aryadi Subagio

Reviewers
John Audi P. Bato
Albert Chen
Diane Mueller
D.M. Noyé
Dan Thomas

Commissioning Editor
Edward Bowkett

Acquisition Editor
Sam Wood

Content Development Editor
Ritika Singh

Technical Editor
Veronica Fernandes

Copy Editor
Karuna Narayanan

Project Coordinator
Judie Jose

Proofreaders
Simran Bhogal
Paul Hindle
Maria Gould
Ameesha Green

Indexer
Rekha Nair

Graphics
Abhinash Sahu

Production Coordinator
Alwin Roy

Cover Work
Alwin Roy

About the Author

Aryadi Subagio is the second among seven brothers. He has loved video games ever since he was little, and he wanted to make his own game in his teenage years. This led him to pursue a Diploma in Computer Programming after he graduated from high school, where he spent years learning about software development techniques. He learned about game development from online sites, because at that time, there was no book on game development in Indonesia.

After graduating, he immediately jumped into the world of game development. During this time, he made a few shooting games for the Flash Platform. After a year, he decided to gain more experience by working in a game studio; this is when he joined Esabra Studio. After working at Esabra Studio, he worked at Enthrean Guardian, a game studio based in Semarang. He has now quit working and is trying to set up his own studio.

Aryadi has a passion for sharing his knowledge. He has written a lot of blog posts about game development on Indonesian and English sites. He also shares his knowledge on his own personal blog at `http://daggio21.blogspot.com/`.

> I would like to thank my mother who supported me while I was writing this book, my brother for letting me borrow his laptop sometimes, and my friends who encourage me.

About the Reviewers

John Audi P. Bato has embarked on a great journey of learning and discovering different approaches of teaching since he started his career in education in 2011. He is currently teaching Information Technology and Computer Science courses at Foundation University at the College of Computer Studies in Dumaguete City, Oriental Negros, Philippines. Throughout his career, he has participated in various capstone projects as an adviser to students with projects related to Educational Game Development and Information Systems.

John completed his Bachelor's degree in Computer Science at Foundation University and is now pursuing his Master's degree in Information Systems at Silliman University as a scholar. He is currently a member of the Philippine Society of Information Technology Educators (PSITE). In 2011, he received his PhilNITS IT Passport Certificate. In 2013, he got certified as an Apple Foundations Trainer, and in the same year, he successfully passed the National Certification exam on Computer Hardware Servicing (NC-2) and the trainer's certification of the Philippine Technical Vocational Education and Training (TVET).

Albert Chen is an assistant professor in the Game Design and Development program at Cogswell Polytechnical College in Sunnyvale, CA. He led students in developing serious games using game engines for the Boeing Company, Neurosky, and Ericsson. His student team won the Boeing Performance Excellence Award in 2008.

Prior to joining Cogswell in 2007, he was a professional game developer for over 12 years, working at EA, LucasArts, Factor 5, and the 3DO Company. He has a Bachelor of Arts degree in International Relations from UC Davis and a Masters of Arts degree in Entrepreneurship and Innovation from Cogswell Polytechnical College.

He reviewed *Getting Started with Clickteam Fusion*, *Jürgen Brunner*, and *Construct 2 Game Development by Example*, *John Bura*, both in 2014 by Packt Publishing.

He is also a reviewer for *Choice: Current Reviews for Academic Libraries*.

I would like to thank my family for their love and support: Joy, Kayli, Brandon, and my mother, Sin Hing Chen.

Diane Mueller is an independent game designer and pixel artist. She has a degree in Game Development from Savannah College of Art and Design and has led and scripted games such as Cadence, which won the Indiebits Gravibyte Award for Humanities, and Five Suns, which won the SCAD Entelechy Best 2D Game award. She has been using Construct 2 for at least 3 years now and has scripted both Cadence and Five Suns, as well as many more games, using Construct 2.

D.M. Noyé (Dwandell M. Noyé) is a successful entrepreneur, conceptual designer, and technical consultant with extensive experience working on major commercial projects with numerous multinational corporations, as well as independent endeavors spanning several fields, from music and literary arts to video games.

I'd like to thank Packt Publishing for once again believing in my expertise and giving me the opportunity to share it on yet another excellent project. I'd also like to thank the entire Scirra Construct community for the deep knowledge base they've built over a number of years, allowing me to acquire the forward-thinking skill of event-based programming.

Dan Thomas is a level designer with a Bachelor's degree in Game Design from Champlain College. He has worked with several teams on QA in the Burlington, VT & Montreal, QC areas, most notably with Birnam Wood Games and their game, Loc, and Minority Media on Spirits of Spring. Most of his work now involves freelance level-design work on smaller projects or games. Dan has worked with many editors and genres across both single and multiplayer games and is always ready for another project or tool to sink into.

www.PacktPub.com

Support files, eBooks, discount offers, and more

For support files and downloads related to your book, please visit www.PacktPub.com.

Did you know that Packt offers eBook versions of every book published, with PDF and ePub files available? You can upgrade to the eBook version at www.PacktPub.com and as a print book customer, you are entitled to a discount on the eBook copy. Get in touch with us at service@packtpub.com for more details.

At www.PacktPub.com, you can also read a collection of free technical articles, sign up for a range of free newsletters and receive exclusive discounts and offers on Packt books and eBooks.

https://www2.packtpub.com/books/subscription/packtlib

Do you need instant solutions to your IT questions? PacktLib is Packt's online digital book library. Here, you can search, access, and read Packt's entire library of books.

Why subscribe?

- Fully searchable across every book published by Packt
- Copy and paste, print, and bookmark content
- On demand and accessible via a web browser

Free access for Packt account holders

If you have an account with Packt at www.PacktPub.com, you can use this to access PacktLib today and view 9 entirely free books. Simply use your login credentials for immediate access.

Table of Contents

Preface

Construct Classic was released in 2007. It was initially created as a hobby project by a group of students working in their spare time. However, the project was really buggy at first, with the team spotting many flaws in the design of Construct Classic, such as absence of support for platforms other than Windows. The team decided that supporting Construct Classic was not a good decision and decided to halt development in April 2013. The entire source code was published on SourceForge, and people can still freely access it if they want, although now there is no official support being provided. Construct 2 was already developed in 2011 with major design changes in mind. One of the design changes proposed was to use HTML5 as the technology behind the tool instead of DirectX that was used by Construct Classic, which allowed the software to support lots of different platforms.

Construct 2 makes it easy for people to make 2D games, regardless of their background. It comes with a complete set of powerful features, has the ability to support multiple platforms and app stores, and possesses an easy-to-understand visual programming system. It is also extensible using a plugin system, with lots of plugins being developed by the community to extend the capabilities of Construct 2.

Learning Construct 2 will introduce you to Construct 2's interface and workflow, and at the end, it will provide you with the skills and knowledge you need to develop your own games, even if you don't know programming at all. This book will guide you through the features of Construct 2, and it uses Construct 2 to create features that are available in popular games, for example, physics, high scores, and AI.

What this book covers

Chapter 1, *Downloading and Understanding Construct 2*, introduces you to Construct 2. This chapter will make you familiar with the interface and terms that Construct 2 uses, as well as give you a quick overview of the event system.

Chapter 2, *Creating Your First Game Design*, will teach you what you need to know about game designing. We will start with the definition of a game, make challenges and rewards, and finally move on to create our game design document.

Chapter 3, *Creating Diverse Player Experiences with a Flappy Bird Clone*, will examine what makes Flappy Bird addictive and how we can attempt to make a similar experience. We will use a technique called procedural generation to create random objects.

Chapter 4, *Making a Breakout Clone*, will teach you how to modify gameplay elements. We will use instance variables to modify the state of game objects.

Chapter 5, *Making a Platformer Game*, will teach you about the physics engine inside Construct 2, how it behaves, and how you can use it to incorporate physics in your game objects.

Chapter 6, *Creating a Space-shooter Game*, will teach you how Construct 2 stores data locally and how to read this data in a game. In this chapter, we will create a leaderboard in our game to demonstrate it.

Chapter 7, *Making a Battle Tank Game*, will teach you about the basics of AI and how to make an enemy object with its own AI. We will make an AI that makes the enemies shoot at the player when they see the player.

Chapter 8, *Debugging Your Game*, will teach you about events that usually cause bugs and how to avoid them. Alongside this, we will use debugging features inside Construct 2.

Chapter 9, *Mastering the Best Practices*, will teach you about the best practices in game development in general and in Construct 2, revealing some techniques that developers use to make their game in an efficient way.

Chapter 10, *Publishing Your Game*, will teach you how to export your game to the Web, desktop, and mobile platforms.

What you need for this book

In order to run the example code presented in this book, you will need an HTML5-compatible browser. Chrome is recommended, though any modern web browser will be sufficient, as they all have supported HTML5 specifications.

To experiment with the code yourself, you only need a Windows machine, as Construct 2 is a Windows-only software. Construct 2 provides virtually all you need to make your own game, from developing to debugging to publishing. The additional software that you might need is a graphics tool such as GIMP or Photoshop.

Who this book is for

This book is for people who want to make their own games but do not have any skills or experience to do so. This book will guide people in creating their game without the need for previous programming knowledge. After reading this book, you will know, understand, and apply the techniques used in game development.

Conventions

In this book, you will find a number of text styles that distinguish between different kinds of information. Here are some examples of these styles and an explanation of their meaning.

Code words in text, database table names, folder names, filenames, file extensions, pathnames, dummy URLs, user input, and Twitter handles are shown as follows: "Construct 2 saves its project in a .capx format, which is just a ZIP file of a project."

A block of code is set as follows:

```
"playerScore1": 50
"playerScore2": 100
"playerScore3" 70
"playerScore4": 20
"playerScore5": 60
```

New terms and **important words** are shown in bold. Words that you see on the screen, for example, in menus or dialog boxes, appear in the text like this: "Clicking the **Next** button moves you to the next screen."

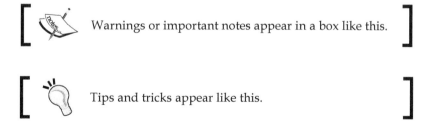

Warnings or important notes appear in a box like this.

Tips and tricks appear like this.

Reader feedback

Feedback from our readers is always welcome. Let us know what you think about this book—what you liked or disliked. Reader feedback is important for us as it helps us develop titles that you will really get the most out of.

To send us general feedback, simply e-mail feedback@packtpub.com, and mention the book's title in the subject of your message.

If there is a topic that you have expertise in and you are interested in either writing or contributing to a book, see our author guide at www.packtpub.com/authors.

Customer support

Now that you are the proud owner of a Packt book, we have a number of things to help you to get the most from your purchase.

Downloading the example code

You can download the example code files from your account at http://www.packtpub.com for all the Packt Publishing books you have purchased. If you purchased this book elsewhere, you can visit http://www.packtpub.com/support and register to have the files e-mailed directly to you.

Downloading the color images of this book

We also provide you with a PDF file that has color images of the screenshots/diagrams used in this book. The color images will help you better understand the changes in the output. You can download this file from: https://www.packtpub.com/sites/default/filesdownloads/7678OS_ColoredImages.pdf.

Errata

Although we have taken every care to ensure the accuracy of our content, mistakes do happen. If you find a mistake in one of our books—maybe a mistake in the text or the code—we would be grateful if you could report this to us. By doing so, you can save other readers from frustration and help us improve subsequent versions of this book. If you find any errata, please report them by visiting http://www.packtpub.com/submit-errata, selecting your book, clicking on the **Errata Submission Form** link, and entering the details of your errata. Once your errata are verified, your submission will be accepted and the errata will be uploaded to our website or added to any list of existing errata under the Errata section of that title.

To view the previously submitted errata, go to https://www.packtpub.com/books/
content/support and enter the name of the book in the search field. The required
information will appear under the **Errata** section.

Piracy

Piracy of copyrighted material on the Internet is an ongoing problem across all
media. At Packt, we take the protection of our copyright and licenses very seriously.
If you come across any illegal copies of our works in any form on the Internet, please
provide us with the location address or website name immediately so that we can
pursue a remedy.

Please contact us at copyright@packtpub.com with a link to the suspected
pirated material.

We appreciate your help in protecting our authors and our ability to bring you
valuable content.

Questions

If you have a problem with any aspect of this book, you can contact us at
questions@packtpub.com, and we will do our best to address the problem.

1
Downloading and Understanding Construct 2

Today's gaming space is a completely different environment from what it used to be. Gaming is no longer just dominated by console and PC games, but has lent its services to other platforms such as casual gaming on smartphones. Today, there are many ways to make games in our modern world, from coding in a native programming language to using authoring tools to make the job easier.

Construct 2 is one of the most popular 2D-authoring tools out there. Its drag-and-drop nature makes it easy to use for people with no programming background. It is so much more than this, however, as it caters to those programmers-to-be with its programming system called an event system, which makes it possible for us to create custom functions. Don't worry though as this event system is easy to understand, and we will talk about it shortly.

Through this introductory chapter, we will cover the following topics:

- How to download and install Construct 2
- Different versions of Construct 2
- Construct 2's objects
- The objects' behaviors
- The project's properties and structure
- Using event sheets

About Construct 2

Construct 2 is an authoring tool that makes the process of game development really easy. It can be used by a variety of people, from complete beginners in game development to experts who want to make a prototype quickly or even use Construct 2 to make games faster than ever. It is created by Scirra Ltd, a company based in London, and right now it can run on the Windows desktop platform, although you can export your games to multiple platforms.

Construct 2 is an HTML5-based game editor with a lot of features, enough for people beginning to work with game development to make their first 2D game. Some of them are:

- **Multiple platforms to target**: You can publish your game to desktop computers (PC, Mac, or Linux), to many mobile platforms (Android, iOS, Blackberry, Windows Phone 8.0, Tizen, and much more), and also on websites via HTML5. Also, if you have a developer's license, you can publish it on Nintendo's Wii U.

- **No programming language required**: Construct 2 doesn't use any programming language that is difficult to understand; instead, it relies on its event system, which makes it really easy for anyone, even without coding experience, to jump in.

- **Built-in physics**: Using Construct 2 means you don't need to worry about complicated physics functions; it's all built in Construct 2 and is easy to use!

- **Can be extended (extensible)**: Many plugins have been written by third-party developers to add new functionalities to Construct 2.

> Note that writing plugins is outside the scope of this book. If you have a JavaScript background and want to try your hand at writing plugins, you can access the JavaScript SDK and documentation at `https://www.scirra.com/manual/15/sdk`.

- **Special effects**: There are a lot of built-in effects to make your game prettier!

You can use Construct 2 to virtually create all kinds of 2D games, from platformer, endless run, tower defense, casual, top-down shooting, and many more.

Downloading Construct 2

Construct 2 can be downloaded from Scirra's website (`https://www.scirra.com/`), which only requires you to click on the download button in order to get started. At the time of writing this book, the latest stable version is r184, and this tutorial is written using this version. Another great thing about Construct 2 is that it is actively developed, and the developer frequently releases beta features to gather feedback and perform bug testing.

There are two different builds of Construct 2: beta build and stable build. Choosing which one to download depends on your preference when using Construct 2. If you'd like to get your hands on the latest features, then you should choose the beta build; just remember that beta builds often have bugs. If you want a bug-proof version, then choose the stable build, but you won't be the first one to use the new features.

The installation process is really straightforward. You're free to skip this section if you like, because all you need to do is open the file and follow the instructions there.

 If you're installing a newer version of Construct 2, it will uninstall the older version automatically for you!

Walking through the installation of Construct 2

To install Construct 2, perform the following steps:

1. First, you need to open the folder where you downloaded Construct 2 and double-click on the installation file. After this, you will be presented with a pop up, as shown in the following screenshot:

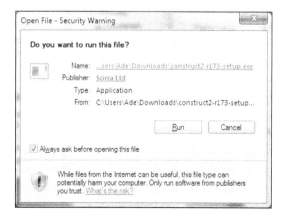

2. This is just a regular security feature; we know that the file isn't harmful to our computer so we can just click on the **Run** button. You will then be presented with the setup pop up.

3. With the appearance of this pop up, the installation wizard has started, so just click on **Next** to continue. You will then be presented with the license-agreement screen.

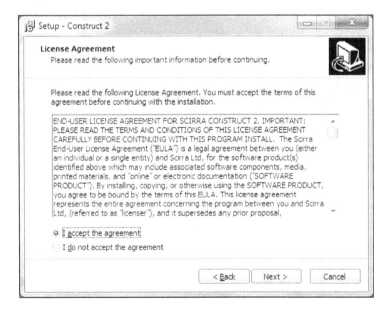

4. The wizard will show you the license agreement; you can choose to read it or not, but you must accept it to continue with the setup.

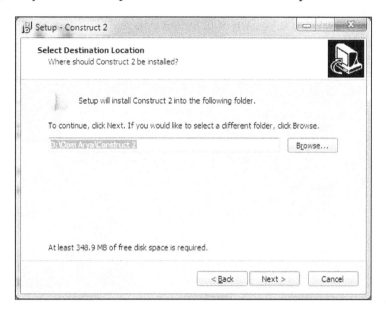

5. Here, you can accept the default setting or click on **Browse** to select your preferred place. When you're done, click on **Next** and you will be presented with the installation versions.

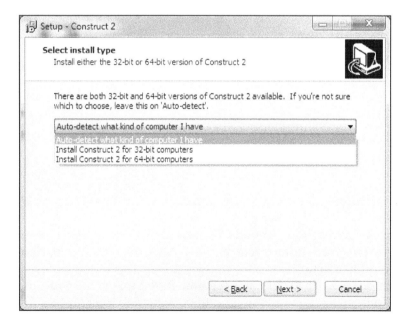

6. As you can see, two versions of Construct 2 are available: 32 bit and 64 bit. You can select which version to install depending on your computer, but if you don't know which one to pick, just select autodetect and let the installation wizard take care of it. When you're done, click on the **Next** button. You'll be asked whether you want to create a desktop icon; check the checkbox if you want to.

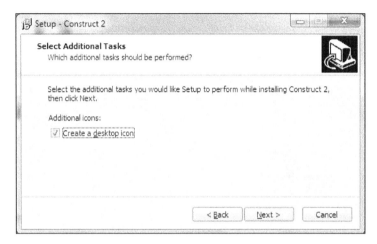

7. After you're done, click on **Next**. The next screen will ask you to install Construct 2.

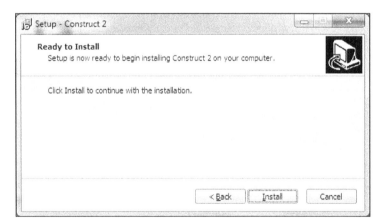

After it's done installing, you can find Construct 2 in its installation folder or on the desktop (if you created a desktop icon earlier). After the installation, Construct 2 will ask if you would like to update your graphics driver. If you don't know whether your graphics driver is up to date, it is recommended that you update it as many issues with Construct 2 not working tend to be related to the graphics driver.

Navigating through Construct 2

Now that we have downloaded and installed Construct 2, we can start getting our hands dirty and make games with it! Not so fast though. As Construct 2's interface is different compared to other game-making tools, we need to know how to use it. When you open Construct 2, you will see a start page as follows:

This start page is basically here to make it easier for you to return to your most recent projects, so if you just opened Construct 2, then this will be empty.

What you need to pay attention to is the new project link on the left-hand side; click on it and we'll start making games. Alternatively, you can click on **File** in the upper-left corner and then click on **New**.

You'll see a selection of templates to start with, so understandably this can be confusing if you don't know which one to pick. So, for now, just click on **New empty project** and then click on **Open**. Starting an empty project is good when you want to prototype your game. What you see in the screenshot now is an empty layout, which is the place where we'll make our games. This also represents how your game will look.

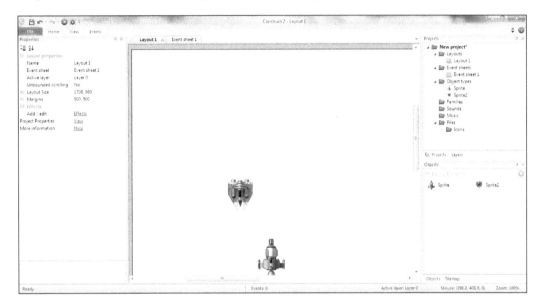

It might be confusing to navigate the first time you see this, but don't worry; I'll explain everything you need to know for now by describing it piece by piece.

The white part in the middle is the layout, because Construct 2 is a *what you see is what you get* kind of tool. This part represents how your game will look in the end. The layout is like your canvas; it's your workspace; it is where you design your levels, add your enemies, and place your floating coins. It is where you make your game.

The layout size can be bigger than the window size, but it can't be smaller than the window size. This is because the window size represents the actual game window. The dotted line is the border of the window size, so if you put a game object outside it, it won't be initially visible in the game, unless you scroll towards it. In the preceding screenshot, only the red plane is visible to the player. Players don't see the green spaceship because it's outside the game window.

[The take-home point here is that the layout size is not the same as the window size!]

On the right-hand side, we have the **Projects** bar and the **Objects** bar. An **Objects** bar shows you all the objects that are used in the active layout. Note that an active layout is the one you are focused on right now; this means that, at this very instance, we only have one layout. The **Objects** bar is empty because we haven't added any objects. The **Projects** bar helps in the structuring of your project, and it is structured as follows:

- All layouts are stored in the `Layouts` folder.

- Event sheets are stored in the `Event sheets` folder.

- All objects that are used in the project are stored in the `Object types` folder.

- All created families are in the `Families` folder. A family is a feature of Construct 2; I will explain this shortly in this chapter.

- The `Sounds` folder contains sound effects and audio files.

- The `Music` folder contains long background music. The difference between the `Sounds` folder and the `Music` folder is that the contents in the `Music` folder are streamed, while the files inside the `Sounds` folder are downloaded completely before they are played. This means if you put a long music track in the `Sounds` folder, it will take a few minutes for it to be played, but in the `Music` folder, it is immediately streamed. However, it doesn't mean that the music will be played immediately; it might need to buffer before playing.

- The `Files` folder contains other files that don't fit into the folders mentioned earlier. One example here is `Icons`.

 Although you can't rename or delete these folders, you can add subfolders inside them if you want.

On the left-hand side, we have a **Properties** bar. There are three kinds of properties: layout properties, project properties, and object properties. The information showed in the **Properties** bar depends on what you clicked last. There is a lot of information here, so I think it's best to explain it as we go ahead and make our game, but for now you can click on any part of the **Properties** bar and look at the bottom part of it for help. I'll just explain a bit about some basic things in the project properties:

- **Name**: This is your project's name; it doesn't have to be the same as the saved file's name. So, you can have the saved file as `project_wing.capx` and the project's name as **Shadow wing**.

- **Version**: This is your game's version number, if you plan on releasing beta versions; make sure you change this first.

- **Description**: Your game's short description; some application stores require you to fill this out before submitting it.

- **ID**: This is your game's unique identification; this comes in the `com.companyname.gamename` format, so your ID would be something like `com.redstudio.shadowwing`.

Creating game objects

To put it simply, everything in Construct 2 is a game object. This can range from the things that are visible on screen, for example, sprites, text, particles, and the sprite font, to the things that are not visible but are still used in the game, such as an array, dictionary, keyboard, mouse, gamepad, and many more.

To create a new game object, you can either double-click anywhere on a layout (not on another object already present), or you can right-click on your mouse and select **Insert new object**. Doing either one of these will open an **Insert New Object** dialog, where you can select the object to be inserted.

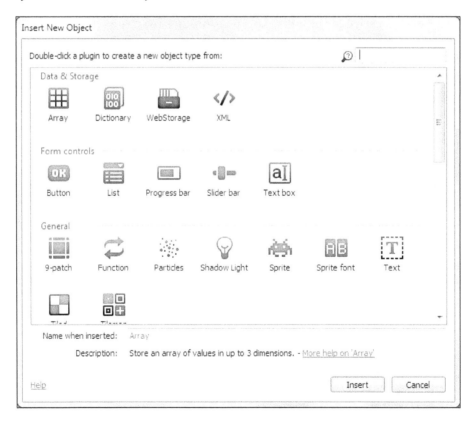

You can click on the **Insert** button or double-click on the object icon to insert it. There are two kinds of objects here: the objects that are inserted into the active layout and the objects that are inserted into the entire project. Objects that are visible on the screen are inserted into the active layout, and objects that are not visible on the screen are inserted into the entire project.

If you look closely, each object is separated into a few categories such as **Data & Storage**, **Form controls**, **General**, and so on. I just want to say that you should pay special attention to the objects in the **Form controls** category. As the technology behind it is HTML5 and a Construct 2 game is basically a game made in JavaScript, objects such as the ones you see on web pages can be inserted into a Construct 2 game. These objects are the objects in the **Form controls** category.

 A special rule applies to the objects: we can't alter their layer order. This means that these objects are always on top of any other objects in the game. We also can't export them to platforms other than web platforms. So, if you want to make a cross-platform game, you are advised not to use the **Form controls** objects.

For now, insert a sprite object by following these steps:

1. After clicking on the **Insert** button, you will notice that your mouse cursor becomes a crosshair, and there's a floating label with the Layer 0 text. This is just a way for Construct 2 to tell you which layer you're adding to your object.

2. Click your mouse to finally insert the object. Even if you add your object to a wrong layer, you can always move it later.

When adding any object with a visual representation on screen, such as a sprite or a tiled background, Construct 2 automatically opens up its image-editing window. You can draw an image here or simply load it from a file created using a software. Click on **X** in the top-right corner of the window to close the window when you have finished drawing. You shouldn't worry here; this won't delete your object or image.

Adding layers

Layers are a great way to manage your objects' visual hierarchy. You can also add some visual effects to your game using layers. By default, your **Layers** bar is located at the same place as the **Projects** bar. You'll see two tabs here: **Projects** and **Layers**. Click on the **Layers** tab to open the **Layers** bar.

From here, you can add new layers and rename, delete, and even reorganize them to your liking. You can do this by clicking on the **+** icon a few times to add new layers, and after this, you can reorganize them by dragging a layer up or down. Just like with Adobe products, you can also toggle the visibility of all objects in the same layer to make it easier while you're developing games. If you don't want to change or edit all objects in the same layer, which might be on a background layer for instance, you can lock this layer:

There are two ways of referring to a layer: using its name (**Layer 0**, **Layer 1**, **Layer 2**, **Layer 3**) or its index (**0, 1, 2, 3**). As you can see from the previous screenshot, the index of a layer changes as you move a layer up or down its layer hierarchy (the layer first created isn't always the one with the index number **0**). The layer with index **0** will always be at the bottom, and the one with the highest index will always be at the top, so remember this because it will come in handy when you make your games.

The eye icon determines the visibility of the layer. Alternatively, you can also check the checkbox beside each layer's name. Objects from the invisible layer won't be visible in Construct 2 but will still visible when you play the game. The lock icon, beside the layer's name at the top, toggles between whether a layer is locked or not, so objects from locked layers can't be edited, moved, or selected.

Sorting the z-order

All objects in each layer are placed based on their z-order. A z-order is the order of positioning objects in a layer. Construct 2 draws objects from the bottom to the top of the z-order; as a result, the objects in the bottom layer will always be behind the objects in the top layer. You can send an object either to the bottom or to the top of the z-order by right-clicking on them and selecting where to send them.

Layer properties

Just like layouts or objects, layers have their own properties. These properties do two things: they change how the layers behave, and they give a good-looking special effect to the objects in a layer. You can see it in the **Properties** bar after clicking on each layer. The members of these properties also have an explanation at the bottom of the **Properties** bar to make it easier to understand. I will explain the ones that are not really easy to understand:

- **Force own texture**: This forces the layer to render to an immediate texture rather than to the screen; this is useful for special effects. The downside is that it slows down rendering, and for most games, it isn't used anyway. If you're unsure which value to set it to, always set it to **no**.

- **Scale rate**: This is the rate at which the layer zooms when the layer is scaled. Set this to **0** if you want your objects' size to stay the same regardless of scaling; set it to **100** to make your objects scale perfectly.

- **Parallax**: This is the rate at which the layer scrolls. The X value is the horizontal scrolling speed, and the Y value is the vertical scrolling speed. Keep it at **100** to make the layer's scroll speed the same as the game's scroll speed. Change it to **0** to stop the layer from scrolling; this can be used for **HUDs** (short for **Heads Up Displays**). With this in mind, a value between **0** and **100** (ideally, **50**) will make it perfect for a parallax-scrolling effect.

- **Blend mode**: This property is like simple effects, as it provides ways to blend the object with the background.

- **Effects**: This applies special effects to a layer; Construct 2 comes with more than 70 stock effects. **Effects** uses a technology called WebGL, or an OpenGL for web platforms, and because of this, it might not available on all platforms. It is already supported on modern browsers.

Saving your project

Construct 2 saves its project in a `.capx` format, which is just a ZIP file of a project. You can rename it to `.zip` and then extract the contents. Construct 2 has two ways of saving a project; they don't affect the game at all, but it is useful to know about them.

- **Folder projects**: This saves the entire project to a folder. This is useful if you're working on a big project with a lot of people in the team, as different people can work on different parts of the game and merge them later.

- **Single-file projects**: This saves the project to a `.capx` file. This is useful if you're working on a small project or on your own, because there's only one file to edit, upload, and share.

What is an event system?

Construct 2 doesn't use a traditional programming language. Instead, it uses a unique style of programming called an event system. However, much like traditional programming languages, it works as follows:

- It executes commands from top to bottom
- It executes commands at every tick
- It has variables (a global and a local variable)
- It has a feature called function, which works in the same way as other functions in a traditional programming language, without having to go into the code

An event system is used to control the objects in a layout. It can also be used to control the layout itself. An event system can be found inside the event sheet; you can access it by clicking on the event sheet tab at the top of the layout.

Reading an event system

I hope I haven't scared you all with the explanations of an event system. Please don't worry because it's really easy! There are two components to an event system: an event and an action. Events are things that occur in the game, and actions are the things that happen when there is an event. For a clearer understanding, take a look at the following screenshot where the event is taken from one of my game projects:

The first event, the one with number **12**, is a bullet on collision with an enemy, which means when any bullet collides with any enemy, the actions on its right-hand side will be executed. In this case, it will subtract the enemy's health, destroy the bullet object, and create a new object for a damage effect. The next event, number **13**, is what happens when an enemy's health drops below zero; the actions will destroy the enemy and add points to the score variable. This is easy, right?

Take a look at how we created the `redDamage` object; it says `on layer "Game"`. Every time we create a new object through an action, we also need to specify on which layer it is created. As mentioned earlier, we can refer to a layer with its name or with its index number, so either way is fine. However, I usually use a layer's name, just in case I need to rearrange the layer's hierarchy later. If we use the layer's index (for example, index **1**) we can rearrange the layer so that index **1** is different; this means that we will end up creating objects in the wrong layer.

Earlier, I said that an event system executes commands from top to bottom. This is true except for one kind of event: a trigger. A trigger is an event that, instead of executing at every tick, waits for something to happen before it is executed. Triggers are events with a green arrow beside them (like the *bullet on collision with enemy* event shown earlier). As a result of this, unlike the usual events, it doesn't matter where the triggers are placed in the event system.

Writing events

Events are written on event sheets. When you create a new layout, you can choose to add a new event sheet to this new layout. If you choose to add an event sheet, you can rename it to the same name or one that is different from the layout. However, it is advised that you name the event sheets exactly same as the layout to make it clear which event sheet is associated with a layout. We can only link one event sheet to a layout from its properties, so if we want to add more event sheets to a layout, we must include them in that event sheet. We will cover this in *Chapter 5, Making a Platformer Game*.

To write an event, just perform the following steps:

1. Click on the event sheet tab above the layout.
2. You'll see an empty event sheet; to add events, simply click on the **Add event** link or right-click and select **Add event**.

 Note that from now on, I will refer to the action of adding a new step with words such as *add event, add new event*, or something similar.

You'll see a new window with objects to create an event from; every time you add an event (or action), Construct 2 always gives you objects you can add an event (or action) from. This prevents you from doing something impossible, for example, trying to modify the value of a local variable outside of its scope. I will explain local variables shortly.

Whether or not you have added an object, there will always be a system object to create an event from. This contains a list of events that you create directly from the game instead of from an object. Double-click on it and you'll see a list of events you can create with a system object. There are a lot of events, and explaining them can take a long time; I will explain them as we go along and create our games in the upcoming chapters. For now, if you're curious, there is an explanation of each event in the upper part of the window.

Next, scroll down and look for an **Every x seconds** event. Double-click on it, enter 1.0 second, and click on **Done**. You should have the following event:

To add an action to an event, just perform the following steps:

1. Click on the **Add action** link beside an event.
2. Click on an object you want to create an action from; for now, double-click on the systems object.
3. Double-click on the **Set layer background color** action under the **Layers & Layout** category.
4. Change the three numbers inside the bracket to 100, 200, and 50.
5. Click on the **Done** button.

   You should have the following event:

This action will change the background color of layer 0 to the one we set in the parameter, which is green.

Creating a variable

I said that I'm going to explain variables, and you might have noticed a global and local variables category when you added an action. A variable is like a glass or cup, but instead of water, it holds values. These values can be one of three types: `Text`, `Number`, or `Boolean`.

- `Text`: This type holds a value of letters, words, or a sentence. This can include numbers as well, but the numbers will be treated like a part of the word.

- `Number`: This type holds numerical values and can't store any alphabetical value. The numbers are treated like numbers, which means that mathematical operations can be performed on them.

- `Boolean`: This type only holds one of the two values: `True` or `False`. This is used to check whether a certain state of an object is true or false.

To create a global variable, just right-click in an event sheet and select **Add global variable**.

After that, you'll see a new window to add a global variable.

Here's how to fill out each field:

- **Name**: This is the name of the variable; no two variables can have the same name, and this name is case sensitive, which means `exampleText` is different from `ExampleText`.

- **Type**: This defines whether the variable is `Text`, `Number`, or `Boolean`. Only instance variables can have a `Boolean` type; I will explain instance variables in *Chapter 3*, *Creating Diverse Player Experiences with a Flappy Bird Clone*.

- **Initial value**: This is the variable's value when first created. A text type's value must be surrounded with a quote (`" "`).

- **Description**: This is an optional field; just in case the name isn't descriptive enough, additional explanation can be written here.

After clicking on the **OK** button, you have created your new variable! This variable has a global scope; this means that it can be accessed from anywhere within the project, while a local variable only has a limited scope and can be accessed from a certain place in the event sheet. I will cover local variables in depth later in the book.

You might have noticed that in the previous screenshot, the **Static** checkbox cannot be checked. This is because only local variables can be marked as static. One difference between global and local variables is that the local variable's value reverts to its initial value the next time the code is executed, while the global variable's value doesn't change until there's a code that changes it. A static local variable retains its value just like a global variable.

All variables' values can be changed from events, both global and local, except the ones that are constant. Constant variables will always retain their initial value; they can never be changed. A constant variable can be used for a variable that has a value you don't want to accidentally rewrite later.

Using a license

Construct 2 has two licenses: a personal license and a business license. If you use Construct 2 without any license, it means you're using a free edition.

The free edition has the following limitations:

- Can't be used for commercial purposes
- Limited to 100 events
- Limited to 4 layers per layout

- Can only have 2 effects per project
- Doesn't have folder organization in the **Projects** bar
- Doesn't have an event search feature

Buying a license removes these limitations. Also, even though Construct 2 can't be used for commercial purposes, it can still be used in educational or non-profit organizations.

The benefits of procuring a license are as follows:

- Buying a personal license gives you complete access to Construct 2's features, without any limitations. The only rule is that once the total revenue that you got from the products you made using Construct 2 exceeds $5000, you must buy a business license. Educational and non-profit organizations can purchase a personal license to remove the limitations of a free edition. If you're a legal business institution, for example an **LLC** (short for **Limited Liability Company**), then you must purchase a business license.

- A business license is only meant for two kinds of people: individuals who have made more than $5000 from their Construct 2 creations or from a legal business. Non-profit organizations never need a business license.

 You can purchase licenses from `http://www.scirra.com/store/purchases`.

Summary

In this chapter, you learned about the features of Construct 2, its ease of use, and why it's perfect for people with no programming background. You learned about Construct 2's interface and how to create new layers in it. You know what objects are and how to create them. This chapter also introduced you to the event system and showed you how to write code in it; the upcoming chapters will explain the event system in more detail.

Now, you are ready to start making games with Construct 2! However, before jumping into this, you need to know how to make a good game. That is why you're going to learn how to make a good game-design document in *Chapter 2, Creating Your First Game Design*.

2
Creating Your First Game Design

Before I guide you through game-development topics in this book, I must first teach you about game design. For those starting out with developing games, this is usually the stage where they say something like "I want to make a game like *Flappy Bird*, *Angry Birds*, or *Candy Crush*", which might not be entirely wrong here, but this doesn't make it exactly right either. This way of thinking doesn't define the kind of gameplay they're aiming for and won't do anything, except reskinning other games that are already published.

In this chapter, you're going to learn:

- What makes a game
- The elements of game design and drawing your game flow
- Game mechanics

Defining a game

So, let's start with a simple question: what is a game? You might have your own definition, or you might have read other people's description of it. There are a lot of definitions of what a game is by some popular figures; a few of them are listed next.

Greg Costikyan defines a game as follows:

> "*A game is a form of art in which participants, termed players, make decisions in order to manage resources through game tokens in the pursuit of a goal.*"

According to Raph Koster, a game is defined as follows:

> *"Playing a game is the act of solving statistically varied challenge situations presented by an opponent who may or may not be algorithmic within a framework that is a defined systemic model."*

Sid Meier defines a game as follows:

> *"A game is a series of interesting choices."*

However, in this book, we'll use my definition of what a game is.

> *"A game is a continuous loop of challenges and rewards."*

While the loop continues, the game will keep on giving rewards to the player. The game can have the same challenges or the difficulty can increase, as seen often. Instead of just changing the difficulty, a variety of challenges can always be supplied as you progress in the game.

Let me give you an example: *Angry Birds*. The challenge here is to eliminate all the pigs using a limited number of birds; the rewards are scores and stars at the end of a level, progression to the next level, and new birds in new stages. The challenge is always the same in the entire game, only more variation is added to the boxes in the level, the number of pigs you need to eliminate, and the type of birds available to you. When Rovio wants to provide you with a new mechanic, they make a new game, for example, *Angry Birds Space*. In this game, in addition to planetary gravity, you also need to think about your movement in space, which doesn't have any gravity at all. Alternatively, in *Angry Birds Rio*, they added bird cages.

 In short, challenges and rewards are the first things you need to design in your game.

Making your own challenges in a game

Thus, to define a game is to define its challenges and rewards, so how are you going to do this? At first you need to come up with a theme for your game. What is your game about? Can you define it in one sentence or even one word? In various parts of the world, even in the Internet, there are events called game jams where people compete to make a game in a limited amount of time. If you participate in a game jam, you will force yourself to come up with a clear and concise idea for a game.

After you come up with a theme, the next part is to come up with a genre around this theme. In games, a genre refers to what the player does, for example, in a racing genre, the player races; in a fighting genre, the player fights; and so on. Let me take an example from a game jam that I recently participated in. The jam's theme was "burning". After I knew the theme, I started making a list of what I can do with fire, such as illuminating something, burning something, or blasting something. I ignored the first one; it is a different property of fire compared to burning or blasting, because burning and blasting destroy, and illuminating is just lighting something. Thus, I ended up with a game that burns and blasts something.

After that, I decide on a *core* that includes the mechanics that make up the player's goals, challenges, and rewards. In this context, burning something means that there is some kind of a track for the fire to burn, while blasting something means that there are targets to destroy. I then created roads for the fire track and monsters as enemies to destroy at various points in the track; this is how I came up with my initial design for a puzzle game. For a puzzle game, what's left is just to make variations in how the track is laid out in each level and how many enemies are there.

Rewarding your players

Now that you've made a challenge, how do you design your reward?

[All rewards must be proportional to the level of difficulty of the given challenge.]

If you made a level-based game, then the more difficult level must produce higher scores after the player completes the challenges in this level, or you can reward players with an in-game item after they complete something. A good way to measure rewards is to keep a record of your result when playing that level. How long does it take you to complete the level? How much of the player's health is left? Is it reasonable? Try changing some aspect of your level a bit and see how it turns out.

In designing your rewards, ask yourself these questions:

- Do players care about your rewards?
- Are your rewards appropriate for the level of difficulty it takes to acquire them?
- Can you give players a choice of what rewards they're going to get?

[If the game you're making isn't level based but just one long level, then the difficulty and rewards must increase over time.]

Game rewards can be in the form of tougher enemies, additional obstacles, new kinds of enemies, and so on. Rewards can come in the form of:

- Something that the player automatically receives in that level (the distance they have traversed in an endless runner game, for instance)

- Something the player has to try to collect to get the score (in platformers, there are floating coins or other things that the player must collect)

- New items after the player has done something (getting a new item after combining some materials in a crafting system)

- Progression after reaching a certain threshold (in **RPGs**, also known as **role playing games**, you level up your characters after getting enough EXP, or experience points)

- Giving the player a means to continue playing (clearing a row in Tetris allows you to play longer)

Rewards don't have to come in the form of a score. Different rewards appeal to different people. Sometimes, new tools or items can give a strong motivation to other players.

Ending the loop

I defined a game as a continuous loop, but this loop can't go on forever; otherwise, we're going to end up with a game that has no end. There are two ways to end a game loop: either the player wins or the player loses. To do this, we have to design two more things: a winning condition and a losing condition.

- The winning condition is the player's target. It is the goal they're trying to achieve in each level. This winning condition can be to destroy all enemies, destroy the boss at the end of each level, or move a character to a safe point without being defeated by enemies.

- On the other hand, the losing condition is the player's threat. It's something they always try to avoid while trying to achieve the winning condition. The losing condition can be when your character is defeated by an enemy, when an enemy reaches a certain point in the game, or when the player fails to fulfill the winning condition in a set amount of time.

One thing to note is that don't just reward your players when they win, but give a small reward when they lose too. This does two things: rewards them for their efforts and encourages them to keep trying.

When making the winning condition for your game, you can choose to design a game, called an endless game, that doesn't have a winning condition. This type of game continues to play as long as the player hasn't met the losing condition.

 Endless games are the type of games that don't have a winning condition; they simply continue on as long as the player hasn't met the losing condition.

An endless game must still have a losing condition and a reward; if not, then the player would have no purpose of continuing to play the game. This reward can either be a score that they accumulate in the game, a new item or upgrades to help players complete a level, or a clock that shows how long they will survive in a level. For instance, consider two well-known examples of this type of game, namely *Jetpack Joyride* and *Temple Run*.

Examples of games for Construct 2

Now let me give you an example of what you can make with Construct 2. As one of the best 2D game-creation tools on the market, there are a lot of genre examples of what you can make with it, such as the following ones:

- Platformer
- Infinite running
- Racing
- Tower defense
- Shooting
- Puzzle

There are also game genres that are hard or impossible to create with Construct 2; some examples are:

- Visual novel
- First-person shooter
- Simulation games
- Massive multiplayer online games

Drawing the flow of the game

All games have a certain flow; this defines what the players can do in a certain part of the game. It is called a game-screen flow diagram. A game-screen flow is an overall flow of the game that shows everything the player can do in the game. An example of a game-screen flow diagram is as follows:

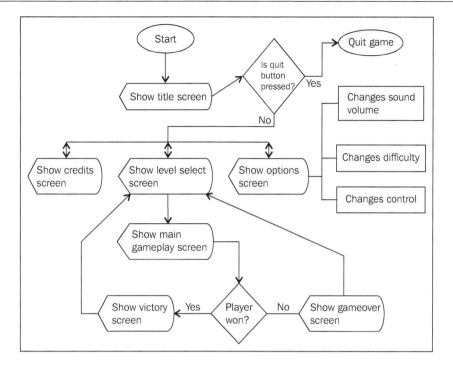

The preceding diagram is a flowchart that represents the flow of a game from start to finish.

It might look confusing at first, so let me walk you through it.

1. Every diagram starts at the... **Start** node (surprise!), and the **Start** node always branches out into one screen, and never more than one.

2. The first screen is what is presented to the player for the first time; in our previous diagram, it is the title screen, but you can show other screens if you want (an intro animation, maybe?).

3. After that, we are presented with a question: does the player click on the quit button or not? If yes, then the game quits; if not, then the game still continues.

This node is called the Decision node, which is a node that always asks a yes/no question and directs the player to the next screen according to the answer.

4. From here, it can branch out into several different screens; what is displayed to the player is represented by the Display node.

If you noticed, the arrows between the screens are of two types: one-way and two-way arrows. These indicate where the player can go from a screen; sometimes they can return to the previous screen, but sometimes they can't.

The reason some screens are not linked by arrows of any sort is because they don't change screens, such as the connection from the **Show options screen node** to the **Changes sound volume** node.

5. Take a look at the options screen; it branches out into three different nodes. These nodes indicate what the player can do inside the linked screen. The three nodes are **changes sound volume**, **changes difficulty**, and **changes game control**.

6. From the level select screen, we can go to the main gameplay screen. However, from here, we can't directly go back to the level select screen; we have to go to a Decision node.

7. Here, the question is has the player won? If the player has won, a victory screen is presented before going back to the level select screen; if not, then the gameover screen is shown.

Remember that this diagram only shows what the players can do and where they can go. It doesn't show what the game automatically does. For example, in the victory screen, the game might unlock the next level if it is still locked, and in the title screen, the game automatically plays the background music.

Making game mechanics

After defining the theme, making winning and losing conditions, and drawing our general flow diagram, now is the time to create the core part of our game design: game mechanics.

Game mechanics define what the players do inside the main gameplay screen, which is shown in the preceding diagram. This is where the players spend most of their time and have fun in your game, and because of this, it is the most important part of game design.

In LeBlanc's MDA design method, mechanics refers to the individual actions the player can take, such as jumping, shooting, dragging puzzle pieces, picking up objects, placing objects, and more (there are hundreds of game mechanics that can be combined in any number of ways to make the next component, dynamics).

Creating game rules

The first step in making game mechanics is to make game rules. Game rules are special rules in your game that might or might not be written in other games. Game rules tell your players what they can or can't do in the game and what the results of their actions are. The following are small examples of game rules along with their game genre:

- Platformers (for example, *Super Mario* or *Rayman*):
    - Players have a set number of lives at the beginning of each level
    - Picking up coins gives players a set amount of points
    - Touching enemies from the side will deduct player's lives
    - If the player's lives are zero, the player loses
    - Touching enemies from the upper side will kill the enemy
    - If players collide with a floating brick platform from below, the players will bounce back down
    - If players collide with a floating green platform from below, the players will jump through this platform
    - Pressing down and jump while on top of a floating green platform will make the player jump down from this platform

- Match 3 games (for example, *Candy Crush Saga* or *Puzzle & Dragons*):
    - Dragging an object will move it
    - If the object doesn't match the neighboring objects, it is automatically returned to its original position
    - If the object matches the neighboring objects, then they're all destroyed
    - Players can move and match as many objects as they want as long as the remaining time isn't zero

- Tower defense (for example, *Kingdom Rush* or *Plants vs Zombies*):
  - There are places where towers can be placed and where towers can't be placed.
  - There are predefined paths for enemies to walk on
  - In each level, enemies come in a few groups called "waves"
  - Towers can be upgraded or destroyed

These rules have been created for the sake of examples; you can write as many or as little game rules as you want. You need to always add at least one rule that's unique to your game to make it different from other games. In the tower-defense example, you can add an element system to add elements to the tower's attacks (such as a fire-based attack or a wind-based attack), and there are enemies who are strong against certain elements. Alternatively, if you only want to make a clone of your favorite game, you could just make slight changes to the existing game mechanics.

Main game phases

This is what happens inside the main gameplay screen in our game-screen flow diagram, from the time the level started until it ended, whether players meet the winning condition or the losing condition. Taking an example from the tower-defense game, the flow will look as follows:

- **The preparation phase**: This is when players are able to place their towers. There will be an information box that tells the players what type of enemies to expect in the next wave. This phase lasts for a few seconds before changing to the battle phase.

- **The battle phase**: When waves of enemies start their attack, players can still place new towers in this phase. This phase ends after the current wave of enemies ends.

  If the level still has any more enemy waves, it returns to the preparation phase; if not, then the player wins.

Depending on what happens to the player during the entire level, certain things can take place:

- If the player was defeated during the battle phase, then the player loses.
- If the player wins, then calculate the rewards to be given to them (this can be from the remaining health, number of towers used, the time it took to defeat all the enemies, and so on).
- If the player loses all their lives, then they receive a small reward for their effort. This small reward can be gold points that players can use to buy new towers that might help them win the level next time.

To create your main game phases, there are a few questions you need to ask yourself regarding the challenges and rewards that you make for your game:

- How do the challenges force your players' skills?
- What can the players do in your game to overcome these challenges? Do the players have a lot of options to use?
- What happens when the player fails to clear the challenges? Can they retry that level? Do they have a better chance the second time?
- Is the reward really worth the trouble it took the players to overcome the challenges?

To make it easier to understand, I have a small diagram that shows what the main game phases in general should look like. You can make this diagram more detailed depending on your answer to the questions posed earlier.

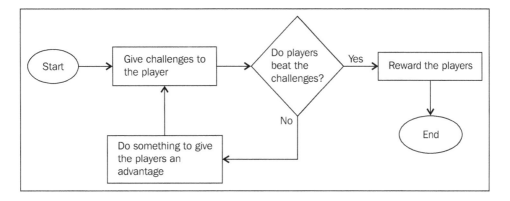

Understanding the fun factor

Now, we are nearing the completion of our game design, but before we can call it complete, there's one more thing that needs to be covered: the fun factor. This is one of the reasons why people play your game, to have fun. Other reasons are to kill some time or as an escape from the everyday routine. I will describe this feeling of fun into two broad meanings: entertaining fun and challenging fun. A game can use one of the two or combine them in a certain way to create their own experiences.

- **Entertaining fun**: This is the feeling we get when we're relaxed and amused; we don't need to try too hard to get this kind of feeling. Games that gives this kind of fun don't give too many hard challenges and are often made with simple rules that are given many variances to each level. These games also want to make the players experience some core feeling such as the cool feeling you get after completing a level.

- **Challenging fun**: This is the opposite of entertaining fun. Games that aim to give this kind of fun use all the game rules they have to push the players to the limit of their skills in order to try to beat the game. Players will get their own enjoyment after they beat the challenges and clear the level rather than from the experience of something fun/cool.

This definition of fun that the game is trying to give to the players is usually not written as a section or a bullet point in the game design, but it is incorporated in the whole design. It determines the kind of visual the game presents and defines how hard the level is. If the game has dialogues, it will set whether there will be comedic lines or not.

This fun factor is meant to be felt by the players, whether they feel joy, excitement, or maybe, the drama in the narrative of the game. Every game tries to give its own experience to the players.

More references for game design

Most of the things, if not all, that I taught you here came from my personal experience. There are a lot of other experts out there in the field of game design; they have their own opinions regarding game design, which I recommend you to look into. I will add some references in this part for you to read.

Game-design template

There is a good game-design template from Bob Bates' book, titled *Game Design: Second Edition*. I will include an example outline (taken from Bates' text, with the non-applicable or complicated parts removed):

- Game Name
- Executive Summary
  - ° High Concept (elevator pitch/"core")
  - ° Hook (what makes the game unique and special)
  - ° Genre
  - ° Visual Style
- Core Gameplay
  - ° List each mechanic the player will do
- Project Scope
  - ° Number of Characters (if there are more than one)
  - ° Number of Levels/Missions/Puzzles
  - ° Number of Enemies (if applicable)
  - ° Number of Weapons (if applicable)
  - ° Etc.
- Platforms being Published On
- Menu Diagrams
  - ° Game Screen Flow Diagram (this is what I explained as "general flow diagram")
  - ° Main Menu Diagram
  - ° Game/Pause Menus
  - ° Win/Game Over Screen Progression
- Art List
  - ° Art
  - ° Sound and music

Game-design books

There are a lot of good game books out there; I will only list some of them here for you to read:

- *Challenges For Game Designers* at `http://www.amazon.com/Challenges-Game-Designers-Brenda-Brathwaite/dp/158450580X`

- *Game Design* at `http://www.amazon.com/Game-Design-Bob-Bates/dp/1592004938`

- *Level Up! The Guide To Great Video Game Design* at `http://www.amazon.com/Level-Up-Guide-Great-Design/dp/047068867X`

- *A Theory of Fun for Game Design* at `http://www.amazon.com/Theory-Game-Design-Raph-Koster/dp/1449363210/ref=pd_sim_b_4?ie=UTF8&refRID=0RF5R20HCRGDSR4JEY0N`

- *Game Feel: A Game Designer's Guide To Virtual Sensation* at `http://www.amazon.com/Game-Feel-Designers-Sensation-Kaufmann/dp/0123743281`

Summary

In this chapter, you learned about my definition of game and how to make our game's challenges and rewards. You learned how to create a general game flow and a main game flow, and you learned about game mechanics. You also learned about two definitions of fun and how to incorporate them into our game.

Now that you know how to make a game design, it is time to make use of this new information by making our first Construct 2 game. We will start by making a simple game that everyone knows: *Flappy Bird*.

3

Creating Diverse Player Experiences with a Flappy Bird Clone

Alright, here we are! In this chapter, we will make our first Construct 2 game using the game design information that we obtained from the previous chapter. We will look at a popular game that everyone knows, *Flappy Bird*, and try to make something similar. We will analyze what makes it good and what can we do to make it more engaging.

In this chapter, we will look at:

- What the *Flappy Bird* game design looks like
- How to make a dynamic gameplay
- How to add modifications from the original design
- How to add collectibles

How Flappy Bird works

Let's first take a look at how *Flappy Bird* works and how it ended up with its designs. The game is really simple; players control a bird that automatically falls to the ground, and to prevent this bird from falling, players need to touch the screen to make the bird *flap* upward. There are pipes coming from the right-hand side of the screen, and there's only a small gap left for the bird to go through.

Everything seems so simple, so how did it become so popular? The answer is through simple controls and random generation. The way to control the game is just through a one-finger tap; everything else (like the bird falling down and pipes coming from the right-hand side) is handled by the game. The other factor is random generation.

Understanding random generation

So, what is random generation and how did it make the *Flappy Bird* experience so engaging?

 Random generation is a technique used to create a game object at a random place or random interval, or the created object itself might be random.

This is what's used when creating the pipes; there is a gap at a random position between two pipes when they are created. Why is this so important? How does this create a challenging experience? It's because the pipes are randomized. *Flappy Bird* creates a different level every time the game is played, so no two playthroughs will be the same. If the gaps are created at a fixed location for every play, players can remember them. Once the players remember them, the game starts becoming less challenging. Dong Nguyen, the game's developer, will then be forced to add more levels with different gap positions.

Flappy Bird game design

Now, to better understand the inner workings of *Flappy Bird*, we will try to make its game design based on what we learned in *Chapter 2, Writing Your First Game Design*. This might not reflect how Dong Nguyen created his game design. The following game design document is written in the way I would write a game design document to make this chapter easier to understand:

- **Elevator pitch**: This is a game where you have to fly a bird through small gaps made up of randomly generated obstacles.

- **Theme**: This is a one-tap game.

- **Genre**: These are casual games.

- **Challenges**: These allow the bird that the player controlled to fly through small gaps at random positions.

- **Rewards**: Rewards are such that one point is added every time they managed to fly through a gap.

- **Winning condition**: There is no winning condition. This is an endless game.
- **Losing condition**: There are two losing conditions: if the bird hits the ground and if the bird hits an obstacle.
- **Dynamics**: This involves the following:
    ◦ The bird automatically falls down if the player does not tap the screen.
    ◦ If the player taps the screen, the bird flies up for a few pixels before falling down again.
    ◦ Two pipes will periodically come from the right-hand side of the screen as obstacles. These pipes will form a gap at a random location.
- **Gameplay progression**: The flow is as follows:
    ◦ Unless the player taps the screen, the bird will fall down
    ◦ As long as the player hasn't lost, the game will create two pipes as obstacles
    ◦ If the bird hits the ground or pipe, the player loses

This is the rough design of the game; we will follow this design in making our own version of *Flappy Bird*.

Making our own Flappy Bird game

We will make a game similar to the *Flappy Bird* design, but there will be differences between *Flappy Bird* and our game. This is because the focus of this chapter is not to directly copy the game, but to learn about the techniques used in it. I will guide you step by step in making it using Construct 2 first, before talking about random generation.

Adding the layers

First, we will prepare our game assets. Game assets are the sprites, music, sound effects, and so on that we use in our game. Basically, we can use any assets we want, but in this book, we will use a free bundle available from Scirra's website (http://www.scirra.com/freebundle.zip); this is free to use as long as it is used with Construct 2. Download it and put it where you're most likely to find it.

Start up Construct 2 and create a new empty project like I showed you in *Chapter 1, Downloading and Understanding Construct 2*. The first thing I do when I create a new project is to set up layers that I will use in the game. This is important because if your game creates new objects on a layer, you need to create that layer first before making the events to create the objects. We will create five layers in total; these layers are as follows:

- HUD: This is short for Heads Up Display; this is the place where we put our user interfaces
- Collectibles: This is the place for coins or other objects
- Main: This is where the in-game-character that the player plays is created among other things that don't fit other layers
- Obstacles: This layer is specifically for things that the player must evade
- Background: This is for the background

The layers will look like the ones shown in the following screenshot:

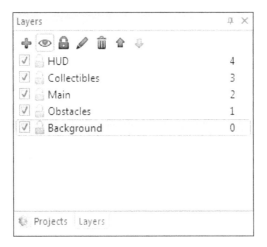

Now that we have more than one layer, I need to tell you about the active layer. An active layer is the layer that's selected last on the layer bar; if you add a new object to the layout, it would be added to the active layer before you move it to other layer. It is also the layer with the properties shown on the **Properties** bar.

 In computer graphics, a sprite is a two-dimensional image that is integrated into a larger scene. This image can be moved on screen and manipulated as a single entity.

Remember that if you add a new object, for example, a sprite, to an active layer that is locked, this object will automatically be locked as soon as it is added. You won't be able to move or resize it unless you move it to an unlocked layer. You can see which layer is the active layer in the bottom-right corner of the Construct 2 window.

Adding a Sprite object

Change the active layer to main by clicking on the **Main** layer in the layer bar, and then, insert a new Sprite object. Change the name of the object to something you want. Although it can be changed later on, it is a good practice to change it first before adding the game object so that you don't have two objects with similar names. Here, we'll name it `bluePlane`.

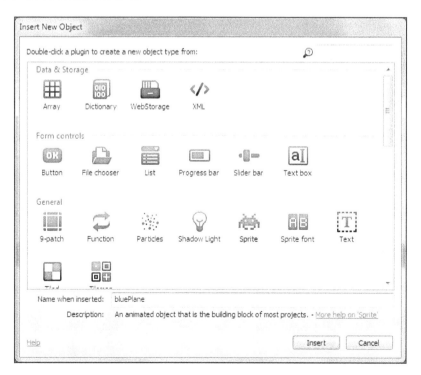

If a newly added object has the same name as an object that's already inserted into the game, Construct 2 will automatically rename it. So, it's advised that you rename the object before adding it.

After adding a Sprite object, you will be presented with an edit image pop up. Basically, its function is to add an image to a sprite, but it is a bit complicated to understand, so I didn't explain it in detail in *Chapter 1*, *Downloading and Understanding Construct 2*. I'll explain it in more detail now.

There are four pop-up windows here:

- Edit image
- Animations
- Animation frames
- The color palette / image points window

The following screenshot is of the edit image window; you can perform basic image editing here, such as drawing, deleting, and coloring, or you can just load an image from a file. You can also set the image points and collision polygon for this sprite here (I'll explain these two in a while).

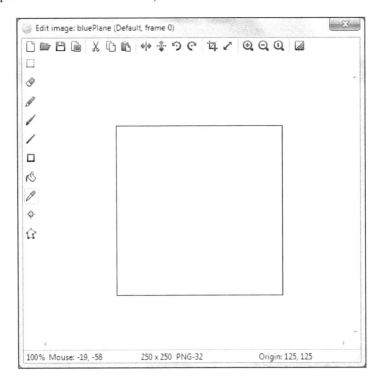

The next screenshot is of the animations window; all sprites are inserted into an animation even if it is only one frame. You can add new animations by right-clicking on this window.

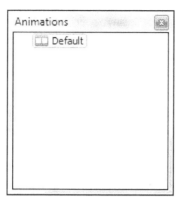

The animation frames window given next shows the sprites for each frame for the selected animation. This is the place to add more sprites if your animation has more than one frame. You can add frames individually or from a sprite sheet.

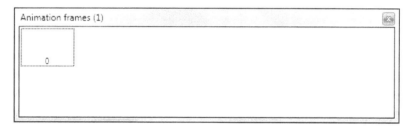

The last pop-up window is the color palette / image points window. These two windows show up based on the tools you clicked on the left-hand side of the edit image window. If you clicked on an eraser tool, these windows wouldn't show up. The color palette window is easy to understand; it lets you select a color to draw or fill a section with. What needs more explanation is the image points window, but before that, let's add an image. We'll add a blue plane sprite from the free bundle package; it is located inside the Tappy Plane folder.

Click on the icon shown in the previous screenshot to select an image from a file. Navigate to where you put your free bundle folder and select `planeBlue1.png` from `Tappy Plane\Planes`. Now I'll explain the image points and collision polygon.

Using image points

So, what are image points? Image points are positions in a sprite that can be accessed from the code. There are two kinds of image points: origin and image points. Origin is the central point of the sprite; it is where your sprite will be placed when you put it in the game, which is usually the middle point of the sprite. While image points are positions in the sprite that can be used and manipulated from code, these are usually used when you want to create something at a certain position from the sprite; for example, you might have a spaceship sprite that can shoot out lasers.

To add/change image points, click on the image points tool on the left-hand side of the edit image window:

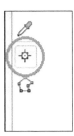

Clicking on this will show you the image points window. This is where you can add or delete image points or change the position of the existing image points.

There are two things to remember:

- Each image frame must have one origin; you can't add or delete an origin.
- The image points for each frame are separated, which means that if you've added an image point in frame 1 of an animation, it's not automatically added to frame 2, frame 3, and so on. However, you can right-click on the image point and copy it to all the frames in the animation.

Setting the collision polygon

There's one last thing I want to cover before finishing this part on adding a Sprite object; the collision polygon. A collision polygon is a collection of points in a sprite that make up a collision area / hit area in a sprite. If another object overlaps this collision area, then it is specified as a collision, or, in other words, when something touches this, it *hits* the object. These collision polygons are created automatically when you load an image from a file.

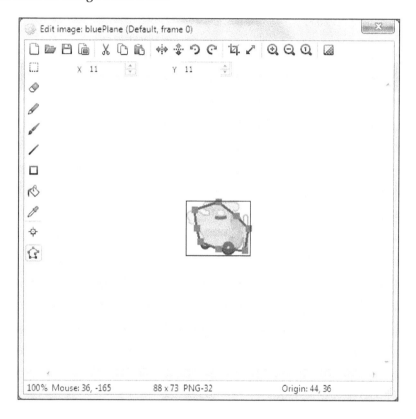

The red squares are the collision polygons, and the blue area in the middle is the collision area. You can move each polygon to make a custom collision area; perhaps you want to make a collision area that is smaller than the sprite.

Remember that just like image points, collision polygons for each frame in an animation are separated from each other. So, if you edit the polygons in a frame, make similar polygons for the other frames too. As with image points, you can right-click on one of the red squares in the collision polygon and copy it to the entire animation.

That's all about adding a Sprite object to a layout. It needs a thorough explanation because a sprite is a complex object; other objects aren't as complicated as this one, and generally, when you want to add them, you just need to click on the **Add** button. Now, just click on the **X** button of the edit image window to close the window and add your object to the layout.

Then, change the active layer to **Obstacles**, because we're going to add the ground and rocks as obstacles. The ground is also considered an obstacle, because if the player collides with it, they will lose the game.

Follow the steps that we used to add a sprite to add a new Sprite object with the `groundDirt` image from the free bundle pack to our layout. After that, add a background to the background layer; you will have a layout that looks like the one shown in the following screenshot:

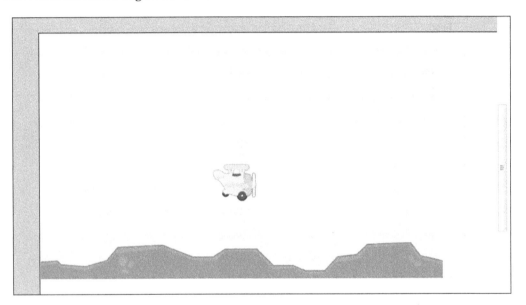

As you can see, there's a small gap on the right-hand side between the sprites and the dotted line; this gap is the border of the game window. To make the sprites and the dotted line fit the game border, we can create a copy of the sprites to be put right beside the existing sprites. A copy of the existing objects is called an instance. Actually, even the original copy is called an instance of an object, so the original object is the first instance of an object, the second object (or the first copy) is called the second instance, and so on.

To make a copy of an object, hold *Ctrl* and then left-click and drag the object; you will automatically create another instance of that object.

After you make a copy, put it beside the first instance to fill the small gap in the game window. You'll see that most of the second instance of the ground is outside of the game window. Leave it be right now, but later we'll make it scroll to the left to make the illusion of the plane going right.

 To zoom in / out on the layout, hold the *Ctrl* key and then scroll using the mouse wheel.

Your layout should look like this:

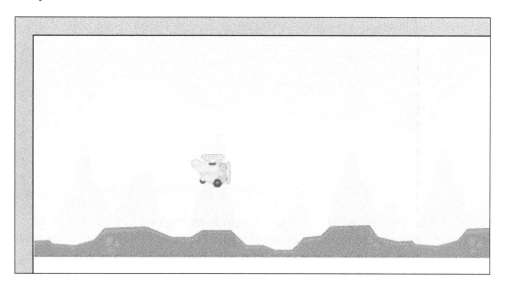

Enabling the plane to fall and collide

Now that we have our plane in place and some ground under it, we can experiment with making it fall. A simple way to do this is using behaviors.

 Behaviors are plugins that are meant to be used by game objects to make them behave in a certain way.

Not all objects can use behaviors. For example, an array object can't use behaviors, but common objects, such as the Sprite object, can. Behaviors can be used to add attributes to an object to make it fade and be draggable or to add movement functions to an object. To add behaviors to an object, first click on that object and then click on the **Behaviors** element in the **Properties** bar to add/edit behaviors:

Clicking on **Behaviors** will open the behaviors dialog where you can see the current behavior for the object and also add behaviors for the selected object. Clicking on the plus sign adds a new behavior, clicking on the pencil icon renames a selected behavior, and clicking on the trash bin icon deletes a selected icon.

Clicking on the plus sign will open another window; this one is the list of all the behaviors you can choose to add. There are a lot of behaviors to choose from, so this might confuse you. For now, just scroll down and find the **8 Direction** behavior; select it and click on the **Add** button to add it.

The 8 Direction behavior is a behavior for basic movements. It allows the object to move in eight directions and rotate around smoothly. Before we move on to the event sheet and write our first bit of code, we should first disable this behavior's default control property. This property makes the object movable using arrow keys.

Since we don't want our plane to be moved with arrow keys, we need to disable it. Select the blue plane and change the property to **no**. This is because, by default, the 8 Direction behavior uses arrow keys to move, and this is what we disabled in this step.

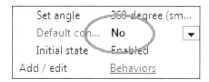

Now, we will make the plane automatically fall down and collide with the ground. Then, we will move to the event sheet and add the code as well. Click on **Add event** and select the **System** object. Double-click on the **Every tick** event. After you create the event, we'll add the action by clicking on the **Add action** link. Select the bluePlane icon and then double-click on 8 Directions' **Simulate control** action. A dialog box will appear where you'll select which direction to simulate. Select **Down** and click on the **Done** button; you'll get the following event:

This will make the plane go down with every tick, which is all the time. If we test it now, the plane will go down and keeps going down until it passes below the lower game screen. This is something we don't want, and we need to add some lines of code to stop it; to stop a movement, we need to disable the behavior as follows:

This event will disable the 8Direction behavior of `bluePlane` when it collides with the ground. To test the layout (technically called "run the layout"), you can press *F5* or click on the run layout icon:

Making it tap to flap

Now, our plane has fallen down and has collided with the ground like we wanted. Next, we want to make it *flap* up when tapped. Translating it to code, the flap is moving up for a short amount of time before automatically falling down again. To do this, we need to add one more behavior: a timer behavior.

A timer is used to count how many seconds have passed since it's started and the object with this behavior will execute some actions after that many seconds have passed. This action can be performed just once or repeated over and over again. To add a timer, just follow the steps you performed when adding the 8 Direction behavior.

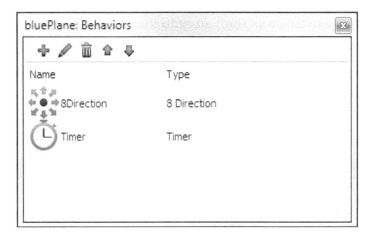

Now, we can start to make the plane flap up but before that we need to add one more thing as a condition to the event to make our plane go up. Earlier, we made our plane go down at every tick, but how do we make the plane go up? The answer is an **instance variable**.

Using instance variables

Instance variables are just like other variables, but they are associated with each instance of an object. If you add an instance variable to an object, this instance variable is also copied over to the new instance of the object, but changing a value of an instance variable doesn't change the value of the instance variable in other instances of the same object. For example, if you're making a shooting game, you can add an instance variable called `Health` to all the enemy ships, but the value of each enemy ship's health will vary based on which one has been shot by the player.

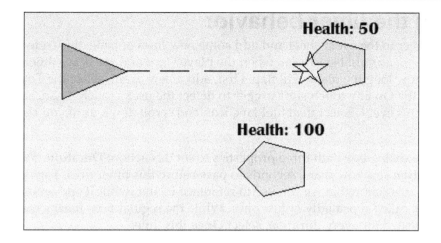

To create a new instance variable, first select an object to which we want to add a new instance variable, in this case, `bluePlane`. Then, select the blue instance variables on the **Properties** bar; this will open up a new dialog window similar to the behavior's dialog with similar functionalities to add/edit instance variables. Clicking on the plus sign will open a new instance variable dialog where we can add a new instance variable. Enter `flapping` in the **Name** field, select **Boolean** as **Type**, and keep the value as `false`. The dialog will look as follows:

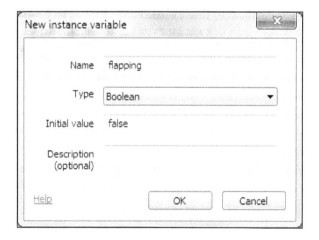

You can add a description of the instance variable if you'd like; after that, clicking on the **OK** button will add this instance variable to the selected object. Next, close the instance variable's dialog window and add a new game object, which is a Touch object. This is an object that's available to the entire project. If the object is successfully added, you will see a notification at the top of Construct 2 saying the object will be available to the entire project.

Using the timer behavior

Now, go over to the event sheet and add some new lines of code; this code will set the `flapping` variable to `true` when the player taps and starts the timer that indicates how long the plane will flap. First, add a new event, select the Touch icon, and select the **On any touch start** trigger to detect the user's touch. Then, add a new action for this event. Select the bluePlane icon and scroll down until you see the **Start timer** action; double-click on it.

You'll see a dialog box with three properties to set this action: **Duration**, **Type**, and **Tag**. **Duration** sets how many seconds to pass before this timer fires, **Tag** specifies the tag for this action that we can use to reference it later, while **Type** sets whether the timer is called repeatedly or just once. While the regular type means the timer will be repeated for every duration, select **Once** this time:

I used the AND word there to indicate that there is more than one action in an event. One thing to note is that we don't want the earlier action to be run only when there's a tap; we also want it to run when the `flapping` instance variable is set to `false`. So, we need to add a new condition to this event. To do this, select the event and press the C key on the keyboard or right-click on an event and select **Add Condition**. This will open a dialog window similar to the one that appears when you add a new event.

From there, select `bluePlane` and check whether a Boolean instance variable is set. So, the event will look like this:

In future, I will also use the word AND if there is more than one condition in an event.

This event is close but not exactly what we want, because we want to check if the `flapping` variable is set to `false`; in the previous screenshot the event is checking if the instance variable is `true`. To do what we want to, we need to invert that condition. Inverting means making a condition in an event to have the opposite value of what's written.

To invert a condition, we need to right-click on it and select **Invert**:

After clicking on **Invert**, an **X** symbol is placed on the inverted condition. From now on, I will write x in the code explanation when I want to say that the code is inverted. So, the latest code that we will add to our event sheet is as follows:

Start Timer "flap" just means that we assigned an ID of flap to a timer we started. We can use this ID to refer to a timer later on. All started timers will fire after a set number of seconds have passed; in this case, we set it to 0.5 seconds. The (once) part in the code means that this timer will only fire once instead of repeatedly.

Before we move on to the next part, we need to change one thing: the first event where the plane goes down. Initially, we made it go down at every tick. Now, we want it to go down only when it's not flapping so that we can make it go up. If the plane goes down at every tick, then we can't make it go up. So, change the code as follows:

Now, we will do two things: define what happens when the flapping instance variable is true and what happens after the flap timer fires. We created the instance variable as an event that will be used when the plane goes up. To make it go up, we just need to simulate another direction again as follows:

Now, the plane will go up after the player has tapped on it, because earlier, we set the flapping instance variable to true after a touch. Next, we will code what happens after the flap timer fires. What we want is for the plane to stop flapping and falling down again. To do this, we will simply set the flapping variable to false:

This will make the plane fall down after half a second after going up. If you test it now, you can see the plane falling down if there's no touch, and you can see it go up if the player touches the screen (in testing, a touch can be simulated by a mouse click).

Stopping the rotation

For now, the flapping action is looking pretty good, but the sprite is not acting like we want it to. It looks down when falling and looks up when flapping. We want it to look to the right at almost all times. To do this, we need to disable the rotation. To disable the rotation for the 8 Direction behavior, we will set the **Set angle** property to No in the **Properties** bar:

If you test it once more, the plane will look to the right of the screen at all times, making it look as if it is flapping correctly. After this, we will create rocks as obstacles, but first I want to discuss the main topic of this chapter: random generation.

Learning random generation

I defined random generation at the beginning of this chapter and now I will discuss it in a technical fashion. We will create the obstacles at a random position on the scrolling ground. So, first we will make the ground scroll.

Making the ground scroll

To make the ground scroll, we need to first make it move in one direction at all times; to do this, we need to use a movement behavior. We'll use a behavior that is different from the 8 Direction behavior; to make an object move in one direction, we will use the Bullet behavior. Add this to the ground object, just like we added the 8 Direction behavior to the plane object. It doesn't matter to which of the two instances of the ground object you add the behavior; it will be added to all instances of this object.

Now, the ground will automatically move, so we will make it move in the direction we want it to. First, we will set the **Set angle** property from the Bullet behavior's property to No because the ground doesn't change angle when moving. If you test the game now, the ground will move to the right; this is because the angle of motion of the Bullet behavior follows the sprite's angle. We want to keep the ground's angle at 0 degrees but change the Bullet behavior's angle of motion to the left, which is 180 degrees. So, go to the event sheet and add the following code:

This will make the ground move to the left, but it doesn't scroll yet. To make it scroll, we have to make a new ground when the ground created last reaches a position where it is necessary for us to make a new ground. To make it easier, the following screenshot denotes the position I am talking about; look at the selected ground, the one with the right-most position touching the game border:

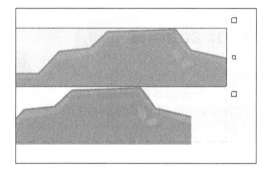

Check out the properties of the groundDirt sprite in the **Properties** bar; the X location we want is 450, so we want to create a new ground object when the object created last reaches this position. The question is how do we know that it is the ground object that was created last? The answer is through an instance variable. Create an instance variable named theLastOne with a Boolean type for the ground object.

Now, we have two `groundDirt` objects in the layout. Change the value of the `theLastOne` instance variable of the right-most object to `true`. Now, when the *x* position of the `groundDirt` object with `theLastOne` instance variable's value `true` is 450 or less, we will create a new `groundDirt` object. After that, we will change its `theLastOne` value to `false` so that it won't create another `groundDirt` object. The code is as follows:

This code will create new ground at the position we want, which is (1220,448). Don't forget to set the Bullet behavior's angle of motion to 180 otherwise the newly created ground object will move to the right instead of to the left. Now I want to explain a bit about how Construct 2 *picks* the target of its actions in the event sheet.

Picking objects for actions

In our previous code, we changed the value of the `groundDirt` object's instance variable called `theLastOne` twice; first, we set it to `false`, and then, we set it to `true`. This is because when we changed the value of `theLastOne` the first time, there wasn't any `groundDirt` object declared in this event block. The `groundDirt` object that is manipulated is the one that fits the conditions written in the event block (the one with the `theLastOne` value as `true` and the X position less than or equal to 450).

After that, we wrote an action that creates a `groundDirt` object at a position we want. If, after this, we manipulate a `groundDirt` object (for example, change the value of its instance variable), the one that's manipulated is the latest one created. As you can see, besides just changing its instance variable's value, we also changed the angle of motion of its Bullet behavior, and the Bullet behavior that's changed is the one from the latest created `groundDirt` object.

That's the basic information about picking objects in Construct 2. There is more to it, but I will explain this as we go along making our game. Next, we will create other obstacles randomly.

Creating random obstacles

First, let's create a new rock object in the **Obstacles** layer; I used the rock sprite from the same free bundle folder. Add the Bullet behavior to it, just like you did with the ground obstacle, and set the **Set angle** property to no so that it won't rotate. Now, put it somewhere off the screen because we don't want it to immediately appear on the screen. Instead, we want it to show up when we create a new ground object.

When we create an object at a random position, we need to remember the range of the position to create. First, the Y position is always at 360 because we don't want to create a random flying rock. Second, the range of the X position is from the left part of the ground object's sprite all the way to its right part.

To create a random value, Construct 2 has a built-in expression called random(), which can be used to create a totally random value or a random value between a range of two values. To create a range between two values, we just need to input the two values inside the bracket, and the expression will pick a random value by itself. The left part of the groundDirt object, when coded, is calculated using *groundDirt.X – groundDirt.Width / 2*, and the right part is calculated using *groundDirt.X + groundDirt.Width / 2*. We will edit the latest written code and change it as follows:

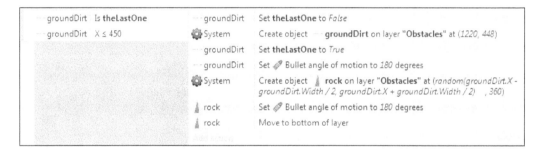

So, we added two new actions: one is to randomly create a rock object and the other is to move the z position of the rock object to the bottom of the layer. We moved the rock object because it looks better that way.

If you test it now, you can see the rocks are created randomly, and you can tap the screen to fly above them; a single mouse click is treated as a tap on the screen. However, you don't yet collide with the rocks; we also want the obstacles to stop moving when the plane collides with them and to make the plane fall down to the ground. To make the obstacles stop moving, we will do the same thing like we did when we tried to stop the plane from moving; we will disable its movement behavior.

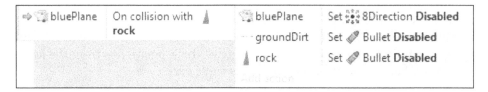

This will make everything stop, but we also want to make the plane fall down. The plane can't flap up after this when the player taps on the screen, because the player already lost the game. We'll add a Bullet behavior to the bluePlane object, but we'll set the **Initial state** property to **Disabled** to make this property not work by default. Don't forget to set **Set** angle to **No**, and for this behavior, set the **Speed** property to 200 to make it slower. To make the plane go down, we just need to enable the Bullet behavior. Don't forget to set the angle of motion to 90 so that it will go down and change the angle of the plane so that it will look upside down.

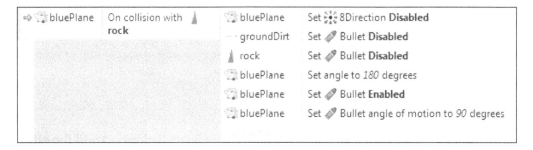

If you test it now, the plane will go down after crashing into the obstacles. Next, we'll add collectibles to make our games more fun.

Adding collectibles

Collectibles are coins or other objects that the players can collect in the game. These collectibles often add something like scores or game coins. In our game, the collectibles will also be randomized. First, create a new star game object with a sprite from `starGold` in the `Tappy Plane` folder and put it in the **Collectibles** layer. Give it a Bullet behavior and put it outside the screen.

We will create new collectibles every few seconds instead of making them every time the game creates a ground object, like the rock obstacles object. To make collectibles, write the following code:

We also want to show what these collectibles collect. So, let's create a new text object; name it `scores` and put it in the HUD layer. Put it in the upper-left part of the screen; this is where HUDs usually are, although they can be in a variety of places. Now, when the player collects the collectibles, we want the collectibles to be destroyed and then add the score. So, create a global variable called `score` with a type of number, as shown in the following screenshot:

Now, add the following code:

The previous action sets the `scores` object's text to a text of `Scores:` followed by the value of the `score` global variable. The ampersand (`&`) symbol can be used to join text with a variable for a dynamic text. If you test it now, you can see the star created randomly, and collecting it will increase the scores. It's starting to look like a game; perhaps, it is only missing a start menu screen. If the stars move too fast for you, you can change its Bullet behavior's Speed property. Just remember to change the `groundDirt` object and rock's bullet speed to be the same value; if not, the star's movement will look strange.

Completing our code

Well, we've made our first game; that's great! However, there are things that are still missing. In a randomly generated scrolling game, any object that gets created needs to be destroyed at some point. If not, the objects that scroll off the screen will take up memory. As more and more objects are created, they will fill up memory space.

So, let's start deleting our objects; first, we'll destroy the rocks. Add a new event. We will compare the rock's X position and see if it is less than `-100`; if this is true, then set the action to destroy this rock:

This will destroy the rock. We'll do a similar thing with the ground, but instead of `-100`, we'll destroy it if its X position is less than `-400`. After comparing its X position to this position, add a destroy action as follows:

Finally, we'll destroy the star. As its size is smaller, we'll destroy it when its X position is less than -20:

Now, we have destroyed all the objects that have gone too far to the left of the screen.

Summary

In this chapter, we created the design of *Flappy Bird*, and you learned how to create a similar game. You learned about the sprite game object in detail; you also learned about two movement behaviors and how to manipulate them in the **Properties** bar and in the code.

You also learned about random generation and how to utilize that technique. Moreover, you learned about object picking in the event sheet. In this chapter, you learned about movement behaviors that we can use to move objects and also learned how to use instance variables in the game.

One thing is still left to be done in our code. If you check the event sheet, you will see that we made all the other objects stop moving when the player hits a rock to make it look like the game stop. However, we haven't made the rock and other objects stop moving when the player hits the ground. Can you modify the code so that the objects stop when the player falls to the ground?

If you're confused about how to write events or what each action does, there are online references on Scirra's website in the manual (https://www.scirra.com/manual) and the tutorials (https://www.scirra.com/tutorials) sections. If you have any questions, you can go to a forum at Scirra's website that helps answer beginners' questions (https://www.scirra.com/forum/how-do-i_f147?sid=14629540d36803dcf68f7ceaf248ab0c).

I encourage you to not just copy what I write here and in the later chapters, but also add your own twist to the gameplay. What more can you add to this *Flappy Bird* mechanic?

In the next chapter, we will use instance variables in a more in-depth way to change the state of an object. We'll do this by creating a clone of a simple game, *Breakout*.

4

Making a Breakout Clone

We created our first game in the previous chapter. If you still remember what we did there, we used instance variables to do two things: flap the plane and make the ground scroll. We used only Boolean type instance variables to do what we want, while there are still two other variable types.

These other types can be used to manipulate the state of an object; if you ever see Mario becoming big after eating a mushroom or becoming invincible after getting a star, then you've seen the example of changing the state of an object. We will create something similar in this chapter.

In this chapter, we will cover the following topics:

- More ways to use instance variables
- What a constant variable is
- What an expression is and how to use it
- How to make an object bounce off other objects
- What sub-events are

Creating the design

Just like the previous chapter, we will start this chapter by making a design of the game we want to make. You probably would have guessed by reading the chapter title that we are going to make a breakout clone. *Breakout* is a game where you move a paddle in the bottom part of the screen to bounce a ball up to destroy blocks. However, some blocks will be able to add some variation to the gameplay. Let's start with the following criteria:

- **Elevator pitch**: An elevator pitch is the description of your game as you would explain it to someone in an elevator, short and concise. This game is a game where players move a paddle to bounce balls off to destroy blocks. Some of the blocks will have special effects to change the balls or the paddle.

- **Theme**: The theme for this game is puzzle.

- **Genre**: The genre for the game is puzzle game.

- **Challenges**: These are used to destroy all of the blocks in a level.

- **Rewards**: Players are given scores depending on what blocks are destroyed and how long they take to complete a level; some blocks will also change the score.

- **Winning condition**: All the blocks are destroyed.

- **Losing condition**: Each time a ball falls below the game screen, the player loses a life; if the player loses all three lives, then they lose the game.

- **Dynamics**: Dynamics are the rules that apply in the game; they form the instructions on how the game is played. For our game, the dynamics are as follows:
  - The ball bounces off the paddle, the blocks, and the three sides of the game area
  - The ball doesn't bounce in the bottom part of the game area
  - The paddle can only move to the left and to the right
  - Some of the blocks will produce a special effect when destroyed

- **Main game flow**: This defines how the game plays from beginning to end, from the start of the level until either the player wins or loses:
  - The ball moves downward at an angle at the start of the level
  - If the ball falls into the bottom part of the game area, the player loses a life

- ° If the ball bounces off one of the blocks, that block is destroyed
- ° For some blocks, a special effect will occur if it's destroyed
- ° Some blocks will need to be bounced off more than once to be completely destroyed
- ° If all the blocks are destroyed before the player loses, the player wins

This is pretty much our design for a breakout clone; we will use this design to create our example game for this chapter.

Designing the reward system

Now, before we actually get our hands on Construct 2, I want to lay out the design of this game in more detail. First, I want to explain the way in which this game rewards the players. The idea I had in mind was to make each block contain a value so that every time it's destroyed, the score will be added by the same value. However, as the number of blocks in a level will be the same for everyone playing, which would result in everyone getting the same score, I decided to add an element to the final score calculation that would vary the score. So, I added the time it takes for a player to finish a level to the score calculation formula.

However, this is still not enough. What if there are people who cleared a level at the same time? Or is it only slightly slower than the other? The gap between each score will be so small that it will be easy to beat the higher ranking player. Also, the skilled players will eventually be able to beat the level in the fastest possible time, making a score limit to the game. To prevent this, I decided to give the game special power ups that can increase the scores. These power ups should appear randomly, and once they appear, they should disappear within a few seconds.

Setting up our layout

Now, we will set up our layout for the game. Unlike the previous chapter where I explained how to add game objects in detail, in this chapter, I will only tell you to add objects when I want you to add them to the layout. I'll only give more details when I'm explaining something new. You can download the sample code from the book's website.

We will use the sprites from the freebundle.zip file, which we downloaded earlier. However, this time, we will use the sprites present in the Puzzle assets folder under the Sprites folder. Open up Construct 2 and create a new empty project. Just like we did the last time, we will add layers to this layout, but now, we will create only three of them:

- HUD
- Main
- Background

Keep HUD as the top layer and Background as the bottom one.

Add a sprite game object to the Main layer and use the paddleBlue sprite from the Puzzle assets folder; this is going to be our paddle. Then, add another sprite object that will be our ball; use ballBlue as the sprite. Now, we have a paddle and a ball in the layout. Next, we will create the border for our level, but instead of using one long sprite to do this, we will create the border by lining several small sprites. This is a commonly used technique when making games.

Making small sprites that will then be lined together is more efficient than making one long sprite, because if you want to make another object that uses the same sprite (for example, with a longer border), you don't need to redraw or stretch it. This will decrease the sprite quality; just line the sprites, and you will get a longer border.

 Lining the same sprites together is more efficient than making a bigger sprite. It also makes the sprites more reusable.

In Construct 2, there's a way of lining a few sprites together, without making the job difficult; we can do this using a tiled background object.

Using a tiled background object

A tiled background object is just like what the name implies. It is a background made up of tiled sprites. If you want to reuse the same sprite over and over, then using one tiled background object is better than making plenty of instances of a sprite object for two reasons:

- **It's easier**: To make new tiles, you just need to drag the tiled background object around and it will create new rows and columns for the tiles; no need to make new instances of a sprite. It's also easier to move the object, if you need to.

- **It counts as one object**: As opposed to multiple instances of an object, this makes it easier for Construct 2 to manage the object technically under the hood and prevents your game from lagging.

 Apart from being used as the game area's border, a tiled background object can be used to place tiles in a top-down RPG / adventure game, or it can be used to construct levels in a platformer game.

Add a new game object, select a tiled background from the **General** section, and rename it as `areaBorder`. You will see an edit image window much like the one you see when you want to add a sprite game object; the difference here is that there's no animation because you can't add animations to a tiled background. You also can't set origins and collision polygons for it. Use `element_grey_square` for the sprite; this is usually for game blocks, but we don't have the appropriate sprite for a border, so we'll use this instead.

 One thing to note is that you can't use any image for the tiled background's sprite; it has to be a square image with a power of 2 as its width and height. A power of 2 in mathematics is $2n$, where n can be any number. So, it's 8 x 8 squares, 16 x 16 squares, 32 x 32 squares, and so on.

Close the edit image window, and we have a tiled background in our layout. You can click-and-drag one of the eight points that surround the game object (you can see it when the object is selected), and instead of making the image bigger, you can actually add more rows and columns to it.

 Using images with the size of power of 2 is also a good habit when creating sprites and assets used in game development. It is a great optimization trick.

Perhaps you've realized this, but when you drag one of the eight points to add more tiles, the newly added tiles are not always at full size, but only a portion of it.

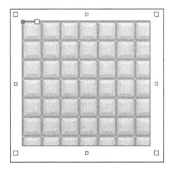

If this is the kind of image we want, there's no problem, but often, this is not the case. We want the object to add new rows and columns exactly by its tile's width or height. Luckily, there's an easy way to do this in Construct 2: by snapping it into grids. Perform the following steps:

1. In the upper part of Construct 2, you'll see three menus near the **File** menu: **Home**, **View**, and **Events**.

2. Click on the **View** menu and select the **Snap to grid** checkbox to snap object placements and resize to the grid.

Which grid? If you want to see the grid, you can select the **Show grid** checkbox. This setting only works per layout. So, if you want to do the same to other layouts, you have to check it manually on each layout.

 To make it easy to place objects in the layout, you can set the layout to **Snap to grid**. Doing so will make object placements and resizing follow the grid.

Now, move `areaBorder` and create more instances of it until it makes a game border as follows:

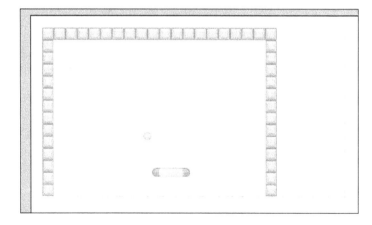

Now that this is done, we can move to the next part of the game: moving the paddle.

Moving the paddle in only two directions

Moving the paddle isn't actually a difficult thing; we can do this using a movement behavior like we did in *Chapter 3, Creating Diverse Player Experiences with a Flappy Bird Clone*. The important thing is that we only want the paddle to move in two directions: left and right. I will explain how to do this by introducing you to another game object: the Mouse object.

Insert a new game object as usual, but select the **Mouse** object from the input category. It will be added to the entire project, so you won't see anything new on the layout. We want the paddle to follow the mouse; if the mouse moves to the left, then the paddle will move to the left, and the same will happen if the mouse moves to the right. However, we only want the paddle to move along the x axis. So now, switch to the event sheet and add the following line of code:

This will make our paddle follow the mouse on the x axis only. If you test it now, the paddle will move like we want it to, only in two directions. However, there's something wrong with it; it follows the mouse even until outside of the game border. This is something we don't want, so we will stop this from happening. To prevent this, we will simply say, "Don't go to the right if you have reached the position I decide." and "Don't go left if you have reached the position I decide." to the paddle. If you translate them into code language, the first event would be as follows:

paddleBlue	X > 576		paddleBlue	Set X to 576

The second event would be as follows:

paddleBlue	X < 128		paddleBlue	Set X to 128

Try testing it now, and now, the paddle only moves inside the game border. We have finished making our paddle move; the next thing we're going to do is move the ball.

Making the ball bounce

We will to do two things: move the ball automatically at the start of a level and make it bounce off objects. These two things can be accomplished using a movement behavior we learned in the previous chapter. We will add a Bullet behavior to the ball so that it always moves in one direction. However, making it bounce can't be done just by the Bullet behavior alone.

If you take a look at the **Bullet behavior** properties in the **Properties** bar, you can see that one of its properties is to bounce off solids, which defaults to **No**. By switching this to **Yes**, we can make an object with Bullet behavior bounce off solids, but what actually is a solid?

A **solid** is just another behavior that can be added to a game object. An object with such behavior is considered a **solid** object, which means other game objects can't walk past it, can't jump through it, and so on. Since we want to make the ball bounce off the paddle and the game border, we'll add this behavior to those objects.

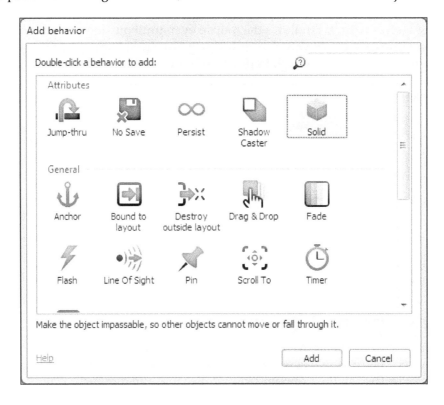

After adding the **Solid** behavior to the paddle and area border, we will have to change the angle of the ball a little so that it moves at an angle at the beginning of the level. So, set it to 45 degrees to make it move to the lower-right angle (or you can set it to any angle you want), and after setting the bounce off solid property to `true`, we are all set. Test the game now, and the ball should bounce on the paddle and off the borders; what's missing now are the blocks.

Adding the blocks

Now comes the time when we need to add the blocks to the game area. Before adding the blocks, let's remember that they have several characteristics such as the following ones:

- They give scores when destroyed
- Most of them are destroyed when they collide with the ball once; others need to be bounced off more than once
- Some of them have special effects when destroyed

We must keep these in mind when making our blocks. There are several block shapes we can use in the `Puzzle assets` folder from `freebundle.zip`, but for simplicity, we'll only be using the rectangle shape here. We'll classify them based on their colors as follows:

- Blue blocks are the normal blocks; they don't give special effects, and they are destroyed on the first collision with the ball
- Purple blocks are the stronger blocks; they need to be collided into twice before they are destroyed, and they don't have special effects
- Green blocks are destroyed on a single collision, but they give a score bonus
- Red blocks are also destroyed on a single collision, and they give additional life
- Yellow blocks give a time bonus on being destroyed

Now that we've planned it like this, let's add blocks to our layout. Insert a new sprite object with blocks with its name, and in the edit image window, load a blue rectangle sprite. We'll also load the other colors in this object so that we can easily set it up and, probably, change it when the game is running. We can do this by adding new animations to this object.

Right-click on the **Animations** window and select **Add animation** to add a new animation, rename it to Purple, and give a purple rectangle image to this animation. Ensure that you click on this animation first before adding an image to it because Construct 2 will automatically select the default animation after adding new ones. Repeat this for the rest of the colors until you have all the required animations.

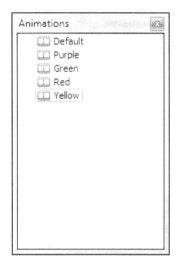

Close the edit image window, and we'll have our block's object in the layout. Next, we'll add three instance variables to implement the characteristics of this object:

- First, add an instance variable named score with a default value of 100; this will add to the score every time this block is destroyed

- Second, add a health instance variable with a default value of 1; this determines how many times the block must be hit with the ball before it is destroyed

- Finally, add an effect instance variable and leave the initial value as 0; we will manipulate this later to add special effects when the block is destroyed

Destroying the blocks

You may think it's starting to get difficult, but don't give up because I'm going to explain everything it in a way that is easy to understand. Now, we can use instance variables to determine which block to destroy, but first, let's put the blocks in place in the layout as follows:

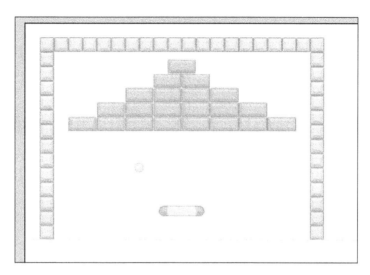

We will first make the blocks collide with the ball and destroy them. Just like the `areaBorder` object, we will simply add a **Solid** behavior to the blocks. This will make the ball bounce off the blocks, but it won't destroy them. To destroy them, we will subtract their health every time the blocks collide with the ball, and after that, we'll check if their health has gone to 0; if it has, then we will destroy them. Translate this into code language, and you will get two new lines of code. The first one is as follows:

The second event will be as follows:

If you test it now, you can see the basic gameplay of the game: you can move the paddle to bounce the ball in order to destroy the blocks.

Setting up the power up blocks

Now, we'll set up the power up blocks at the beginning of a level. There are two ways to do this: set it randomly or define it manually. We'll do it manually in this example, because this kind of game is usually level-based. To do this, we'll first add an instance variable to the blocks called `blockColor` (it's actually a `Text` variable) and leave the initial value to empty. We'll use this instance variable to determine what kind of block it is.

After adding this instance variable, close the instance variable window and select the block whose color you want to change. Then, in the **Properties** bar, change the value of `blockColor` to a color you want. The color must be one of the animations we set earlier, and when you set a `Text` variable in the **Properties** bar, you don't need to type the quote symbol. If you set a purple block, don't forget to change the `health` variable as well, so it needs two collisions to destroy it.

Instance variables	
scores	100
health	2
effect	0
blockColor	Purple
Add / edit	Instance variables

However, just because we change an instance variable, it doesn't mean the blocks' animation will immediately change. We need to add something on the event sheet. We want the game to check the `blockColor` instance variable at the start of the level and then change the blocks' animation to that color. So, we will simply add the following line:

Perhaps, you've realized that there are blocks with their `blockColor` instance variable values empty, but their color is blue. This is because when Construct 2 doesn't find a matching animation, it reverts to the default color, which is blue.

Writing an expression

In the code we wrote previously, we used an expression to retrieve a value of an instance variable.

 An expression is any legal mathematical combination that represents a value. All Construct 2 objects have their own expressions.

One of those mathematical combinations is a variable, so a single instance variable also counts as an expression. For example, you can retrieve an object's position from its x and y values. You can also perform mathematical operations in an expression, such as addition, subtraction, multiplication, and division.

Understanding constant variables

Now, we will start changing the game state. We will do this by utilizing two kinds of variables: instance variables and global variables. We'll make several global variables that will be checked later with an instance variable. However, we will change the global variable to a special type of variable: **constant variable**.

 So, what are constant variables? They are variables, global or local, whose values do not change after they are declared. Both the text and number type variables can become constant variables. To make a constant variable, just select the **Constant** checkbox when creating a new global variable. Constant variables in the event sheet are indicated by their names, which appear capitalized.

Let's try it now. Go to the event sheet and create a few variables needed to create the blocks' special effect. As you remember, the default value for the blocks' effect instance variable is 0; so we'll make a value of zero when the block has no special effect at all. Then, we'll set incrementing values for the other special effects, as shown in the following screenshot:

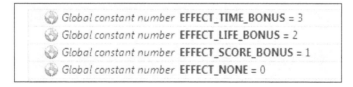

This is the bonus that players get when a certain block is destroyed. So, let's change the value of the effect property of the blocks in the layout. Give a value of 1 to the green blocks, 2 to the red blocks, and a value of 3 to the yellow blocks.

Adding sub-events

Now that we've assigned values to the effect property, we can start adding code to the event sheet. The logic is if the block is destroyed, we'll check the value of its `effect` instance variable; if it is the same as one of the constant effect global variables, we'll change the value of a variable depending on the effect. To do something when an object is destroyed, we will use the `On destroyed` event. Let's add an `On destroyed` event to the event sheet.

Now, we want to compare the value of an instance variable after an `On destroyed` event; this means that we want to create an event inside another event, or in other words, we want a sub-event. To create a sub-event, first select the event you want to make a sub-event from and then press *S* on your keyboard. A new window will open up; here, you can select a new event for the sub-event. Create your sub-event until it looks like this:

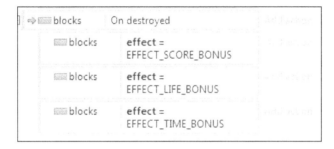

Once again, because adding an image every time I teach you a code will be troublesome, this is how I write it in the code form:

Note that there's no limit on how many sub-events can be made inside an event. You can create a sub-event inside a sub-event, but it is suggested that you do not make too many sub-events because the code will be too confusing to understand.

Now, to make these blocks really work, we need to make three global variables: `score`, `life`, and `gameTime`; all are number types. For life and time bonuses, we want them to increase after a fixed number; life will increase by 1, and time will increase by 10 seconds. For score bonuses, we'll use a simple formula to make it vary per player. The score bonus will be based on the player's life and the current time remaining; the code will be as follows:

We have successfully added special effects that give a bonus when the blocks are destroyed. Now, what if we want to change something about the paddle when a block is destroyed?

Changing a game object's state

Other than adding bonuses to the game, we can make a special effect that changes the state of an object. In this example, we will change the state of the paddle. While changing the state of the paddle, we will determine the duration of the new state, and after this duration ends, the paddle will revert to its original state. To make it simple, the duration of this new state stays until the player destroys another block that doesn't have a special effect. For now, we'll make the paddle wider.

To do this, we'll create a `Text` type instance variable called `state` on `paddleBlue`. The value of this instance variable will determine the state of the `paddleBlue` object. Now, we need a place to change it; let's change it when the purple block is destroyed, because right now, nothing happens when we destroy it.

To select a purple block, we'll take a look at its `blockColor` instance variable; if it says purple, then we got the block we want. After that, we can change the state of this block. One more thing we want to do is change the `paddleBlue` state back to its default value. We can do this by checking both the effect and the `blockColor` instance variable to find a block that isn't purple and has no effect. So, we will add these sub-events to the latest written code:

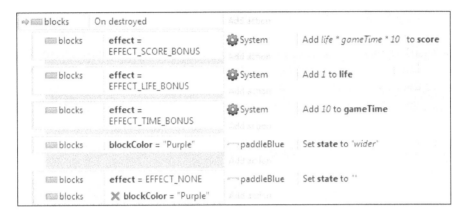

We have changed the state of the `paddleBlue` object; now, to make this really work, we need to add two more events: one when the state instance variable's value is wider and another when it is an empty string. We want to make it wider when the state is wider and return the width to normal when it is an empty string. Note that that the `paddleBlue` object's normal width is 104 pixels wide, and we want to make the width 184 pixels wide when it's wider (or you can set your own value). The first event will be as follows:

The second event will be as follows:

If you test the game now, you can see that the paddle becomes wider after the purple block is destroyed and reverts to normal when the blue block is destroyed, but the paddle stays wide when the destroyed block is not blue.

Adding more states

You already know how to change a state of an object and revert it to its original state. However, what happens when you add state-changing blocks? We'll answer this by giving another state to the paddle. First, let's add another animation called `Grey` to the block's object; give this animation a gray rectangle sprite.

Just like we did earlier, for some blocks, change the `blockColor` instance variable's value to `Grey`. We want to change the angle of the paddle after the player destroys this block, so first, we will add another sub-event when the block is destroyed.

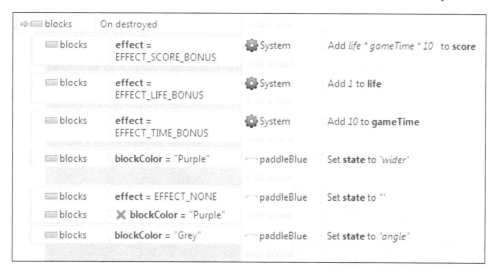

Just like we did earlier, to actually make the state have an effect, we will make another event that checks the `paddleBlue` state. This new event will set the angle of the paddle if the state value is `angle`:

Don't forget to change the angle back to `0` degrees when the state is empty again:

| paddleBlue state = "" | paddleBlue | Set width to 104 |
| | paddleBlue | Set angle to 0 degrees |

Test your game now; if you destroy the purple block and then the grey block, or the other way around, you'll find that the paddle becomes big and tilted at 45 degrees. This is because two effects of state-changing blocks are applied.

As you can remember, we only changed the width and angle of the paddle back to its original value when the state instance variable is an empty string. This time, the state instance variable didn't have a chance to become empty before the state change, thus applying two state changes at the same time.

When making your game, always look out for small gotchas like this. This is because Construct 2 doesn't always know what you want to do, which is a common thing when making a game, no matter what tool you use. This usually happens when you change the value of a variable.

To fix this, we need to deactivate other state-change effects when we switch to a new state. We'll set the angle to 0 when we make the paddle wider, and we'll change the width back to the original one when we tilt the angle. So, we'll add two new actions to two different events. The first event will be as follows:

paddleBlue	state = "wider"	paddleBlue	Set width to *184*
		paddleBlue	Set angle to *0* degrees

The second event will be as follows:

paddleBlue	state = "angle"	paddleBlue	Set angle to *45* degrees
		paddleBlue	Set width to *104*

Ending a game

We have done a lot of things in this chapter, and I have explained many things. I am afraid this chapter is a bit hard to understand. Don't give up, and don't stop because we are nearing the end of the chapter. Now that we have added our state-change feature, it is time to apply a losing condition to the game. There are two losing conditions in this game: when the player loses all lives and when the time runs out. To do this, we'll give default values to the global variables related to the losing conditions. We'll give three lives and start the time countdown at 60 at the start of the level, like this:

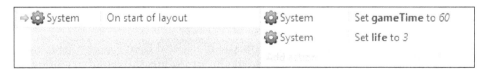

⇒ System	On start of layout	System	Set **gameTime** to *60*
		System	Set **life** to *3*

Then, we'll represent these values on screen like we did in our first game. So, we'll create two new `Text` objects to be put on the HUD layer, name them `txtTime` and `txtLife`, and make their values show `gameTime` and life instance variables as follows:

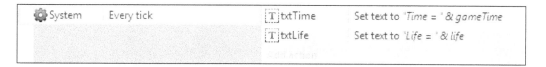

To show that the player has lost, we will display **GAME OVER** text in large when one of the losing conditions is met. So, create another `Text` object called `txtGameOver`, add it on the HUD layer, give it the `GAME OVER` text, and change the font to make it bigger.

To change the size of a text, we will change the **Font** property on the `Text` object. When you click on the **Font** property, you'll see a small box with three dots on it; clicking on this will open a window where you can change the font:

In the new window, you'll be able to change the font type, font style, and font size. Set the new size to 36 and put it off screen. We'll also change the color of the text; to do this, click on the **Color** property of the text, and you'll see a small box on the right-hand side. Click on it, and a box with lots of colors to choose from will pop up. For now, make the **GAME OVER** text red. Move the `txtGameOver` object off the screen, because we will only need it when the player loses.

Losing by time

The first losing condition we want to make is losing by time. The logic is simple: if the `gameTime` global variable drops below 1, which can mean 0 or a negative value, then we'll show the **GAME OVER** text in the middle of the game area. We must also stop the movement of the ball, because we don't want it to keep moving and bouncing around when the player is declared lost. If we write this in code form, it would be as follows:

I want to tell you something about how Construct 2 creates an object. When you want to create an object, this object must already be put in a layout. Any layout is fine; it doesn't have to be the layout that the object is created in. This is because when Construct 2 creates an object, it needs to know the default properties of the object. If it's a Text object, then Construct 2 needs to know the initial text value, color, font style, font size, and so on. It is advised that you have a separate layout specifically to place objects.

> When creating an object, this object must be put somewhere in a layout. It is advised that you have a layout only to store game objects. Another reason to do this is because even off-screen assets in your starting layout will instantiate themselves when the layout started. If you're not careful, you can have a bullet dashed from one side of the screen to the other at the start of the game.

Now, the only thing that's missing is that we still haven't reduced gameTime; thankfully, Construct 2 has an event that does something every second (or every few seconds, depending on what you want):

Losing by life

Now, we'll make the player lose by life. Players initially have three lives; every time the ball falls below the screen, we'll reduce the player's life by 1, and if the life goes down to 0, we can say that the player lost. The question is how does the game continue after the ball falls below the screen. The answer is: we will create a new ball.

So, the logic is like this: if the ball falls below the screen, we'll reduce the player's life by 1; if it is still above 0, then we'll create another ball to continue playing; and if it is 0, then the player loses. So, this is going to be as follows:

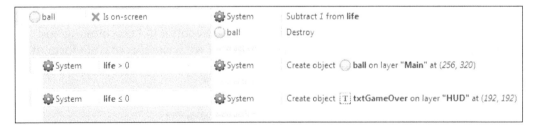

If you test it now, the game should be working as we want it to. However, there's still one thing missing: the score. So, let's make this.

Calculating the score

Calculating the score is really easy because we already have an instance variable in the `blocks` object that we can use to increment the score when it's destroyed. So, we'll basically just add the `score` global value every time a block is destroyed:

Here, we will make a new block, an `On destroyed` event, besides the previous one we made. It's okay to make several events, which are the same as this one; this can be used to chop down the number of actions in an event to make the code easier to read and understand.

 You can create two or more events from the same event. Use this to group actions and sub-events that do the same thing to make the code easier to read and understand.

After we have made the code, it's time to show the score. We'll show it when the level ends, that is, either the player wins or loses. We'll create a new `Text` object called `txtScore` on the HUD layer, and we'll put it off the screen somewhere. First, let's show this object when the losing condition is met. Create a new `txtScore` object when either `gameTime` is below `1` or when the player's life is equal to or less than `0`. So, we'll add an action to two events.

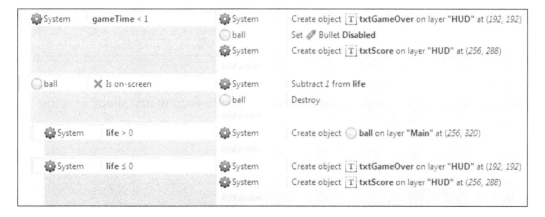

After creating the text score object, we will make it show its initial value. This initial value is not the one we set in its **Properties** bar, but will be based on the score global variable. As a result of this, we'll create its initial value at another place when it is created. Construct 2 has an `On created` event that fires when an object is first created; we'll set the initial value there:

Test the game now. You'll see that the **Score** textbox shows up along with the **GAME OVER** text when the player's life is 0. Next, we'll show the score when the player wins.

Comparing an expression

A player wins this game when all the blocks in a level are destroyed. To know whether all the blocks have been destroyed or not, we will count the number of instances of the block. If it's 0, then we know that all the blocks have been destroyed. Construct 2 has an expression to count the number of instances of an object; to compare an expression instead of a variable, we'll use the system's `compare two values` event, and create a condition `"System blocks.Count = 0"`.

Also, we only want to count the blocks when the game is going on, not after the game is over. So, we'll add another condition that will serve as a marker when the game is over. We want to stop the movement of the ball after the player wins, so let's use this as a marker and set the ball's speed to `0`. We'll stop the ball's movement when the player wins; with actions and conditions combined together, our code will look like this:

Play the game until you win, and you can see that the score is shown as we wanted it to. The ball has also stopped moving, so we don't have to worry about it falling below the game area after we win.

Killing the bug

Well, we've got a perfect working small game. Awesome, right! However, just like any other game, this one potentially has bugs. There are two bugs here: the timer doesn't stop when the game ends, and the timer can count down to below 0. We can fix the first bug by making sure that we only subtract the gameTime variable while the game is still on, in other words, when the player's life and number of blocks are more than 0.

The second bug is fixed simply by changing the text value when gameTime is less than 1. The resulting code is as follows:

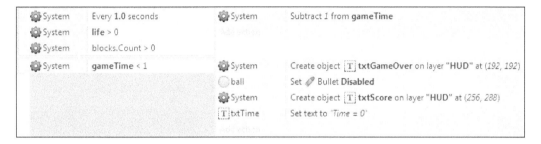

Summary

In this chapter, you learned about a new object, the tiled background, and how to use it. You learned about a new **Solid** behavior and how to use it to bounce off objects. You also learned about expressions, how to use them, and how to compare them like instance variables. You learned about constant variables and how to use them to change the state of an object. Moreover, you also learned about sub-events for the first time.

In our next chapter, I will introduce you to the Physics object and a few things you can make with it.

5
Making a Platformer Game

Welcome to this chapter! We covered a lot in the previous chapter: a new game object, a new behavior, sub-events, and an expression. These new things are among the most common ones you'd use in your project, no matter what game you want to make. Solid objects are used when you want to make obstacles and/or levels in your game, and expressions and sub-events are often used when you're making games with complex mechanics.

I will teach you to use the knowledge that you have gained until now to the next level: how to create a more complex game, a genre that's one of the most popular ones right now, and that's a platformer. We will use solid objects to design a level, and we'll create a Mario-esque coin box and a puzzle element. I will also teach you how to use physics in Construct 2.

In this chapter, we will learn:

- How to prepare a level
- How to use physics
- How to join two objects

Preparing the level

Starting from this chapter, I will skip the game-designing part and immediately get down to the technical bits. This way, I can give you more detailed explanations about each topic. For now, let's create a new empty project on Construct 2 and a level like the one shown in the following screenshot:

This example level has all the basic needs of a platformer level. It has a ground to walk on, platforms to step on, and a floating box that contains a coin. It's a good habit to prototype game mechanics early on, so make the game space capable of testing out either one or all your systems quickly. All the sprites we use here are from the `freebundle.zip` folder under `Sprites\Platformer pack\Base pack\ Tiles`. The `Platformer pack` folder has a lot of sprites fit for a platformer game; it is a good idea to use them in your game sometime in the future. There's one thing missing though: the character.

Setting up the character

Setting up our main character requires us to make a few animations with their own sprites. The required animations are:

- Standing
- Walking
- Jumping
- Hurt

These are just the basic animations; we might need to add more animations if needed, for example, to climb or swim. The character sprites that we will use are available at `Platformer pack\Extra animations and enemies\Alien sprites`; here, there are several ready-to-use aliens, along with their animations. We'll use the green alien sprites in this chapter, but you can use whichever color you like.

Add a new sprite game object and name it `alien`. We'll give it a few basic animations as follows:

For the **Default** animation, we'll use the stand sprite (`alienGreen_stand.png`). For the **Walking** animation, we'll use two walking sprites of the alien sprite (`alienGreen_walk1.png` and `alienGreen_walk2.png`). If we want to give more than one frame to an animation, we would need to use the Animation frames window. For the first frame, add the `walk1` sprite as usual, but for the frames after this one, we will right-click on the Animation frames window and click on the **Add frame** option.

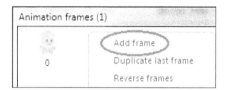

After we add a frame, we just need to load an image from a file. Now that this animation already has more than one frame, the animation will automatically start when we switch to the **Walking** animation. The problem is that we want this **Walking** animation to loop, not just stop after playing its last frame (like all default animations do). So, how do we do this?

The answer is by changing its property. Click on the name of an animation whose properties you want to change in the **Animations** window, and then take a look at the **Properties** bar. You can see that the **Properties** bar now shows the properties of the animation you selected. Change the **Loop** property to **Yes**, and then, this animation will automatically loop after it reaches its last frame.

We are now done adding frames to the **Walking** animation. Switch on to the **Jumping** animation and give it the jump image (`alienGreen_jump`). Close the edit image window, and we now have our character on the screen.

Moving the character

We now have our character on screen, but right now our character still can't move; we'll make it move as if it's aware that it is an object in a platformer game. Thankfully, there's an easy way to do this in Construct 2: using a Platform behavior. The Platform behavior is located at the movement section when you add the behavior. Add this behavior to the alien object, and it can move as if it's Mario. However, before it's able to do this, we need to define the ground for it. An object with a Platform behavior can't walk through any solid objects; so we'll add a Solid behavior to the `grassMid` object. Test the game now, and you can move your alien with the arrow keys.

Changing the animations

I'm sure you have realized that when you move the alien object, it doesn't animate. It still shows its default animation. Well, this is because we haven't told it to change its animation. So, let's do that now.

To do this, we need to be able to detect whether the arrow keys are pressed or not. Construct 2 does this via its Keyboard game object; so, add this game object to your project. After that, change to the event sheet.

We want to switch the animation to **Walking** when we press the right or left arrow key and switch to **Jumping** when we jump and return to the default animation when we're not pressing anything. The combination of the Keyboard object and the Platform behavior has got this logic covered. We will change the animation to the **Walking** animation when the right or left arrow key is pressed; the code for the right arrow key event looks like this:

The code for the left arrow key event looks like this:

Then, we'll change the animation to the **Jumping** animation when our alien is in the air. Luckily, Construct 2's Platform behavior gives us easy ways to look for several states of the character, from jumping and falling to landing. Here, we'll change the animation when our character jumps:

What's left is to change the animation back to the default standing animation. There are two places where we can change this: when the player releases the left or right arrow key and when our character lands after jumping.

The Keyboard object has an On released event to check whether the player has released a key, and the Platform object has an On landed event to check whether the player has landed after jumping or not. However, we only change back to the default animation if the animation currently playing is the **Jumping** animation. This is because we can still move the character even if it's in the air, and we might want him to continue walking to one side right after landing. So, the code will look like this:

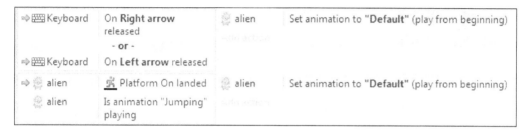

You might have observed the or keyword in the code snippet in the previous screenshot. Just like any other programming language, Construct 2 has the AND and OR keywords, which function as follows:

- AND: This keyword means that all the conditions in an event must be true for the sub-events to run
- OR: This keyword only needs one of the conditions to be true

To make an Or block, right-click on an event and select the **Make 'Or' block** option; the Or keyword will be applied to that block.

Keep in mind that an event can't be an AND block and an OR block at the same time; it must always be one of the two. If you need to look for two conditions at once and then use an OR block, use a sub-event.

Test the game now, and you can see that the character can move using directional arrow keys. However, there's one problem: if we press the left arrow key, it moves backwards! Well, this is because we haven't flipped the image.

There are two kinds of flipping in Construct 2: flipping horizontally and flipping vertically. Flipping horizontally is called mirrored, and flipping vertically is called flipped. Here, we want to mirror the sprite when we press the left arrow key and unmirror it when we press the right arrow key. Change the code to look like this when we are setting the animation to **Walking**:

The code looks like this for the left arrow key event:

This will make our character face left when we press the left arrow key and face right when we press the right arrow key. Don't forget to save your project before moving on to the next part.

Making the camera follow the player

By now, the alien can move normally. However, if you try to move past the right-hand side of the screen, the player disappears! This is because the camera stays still while the player moves to the right, To fix this, we will make the camera follow the player.

It might sound difficult, but we actually only need to add one new behavior to the player: the Scroll To behavior. This behavior will force the camera to stick to the object with this behavior, or if there is more than one object with this behavior, it will stick to the center, between all the objects. Add this behavior, and the camera will automatically follow the player.

There's one more problem I want to address here while we're still in the topic of moving the character. If you walk too far to the left or right part of the layout, you can see that the alien can fall out of the layout. This is because there isn't anything that prevents the player from falling. There are two ways to prevent this: build a wall of solid objects on both sides of the layout or just use a behavior to stop the object from going out of the layout.

This behavior is called Bound to Layout. All objects with this behavior can't go out of the layout, as if there are invisible walls that prevent them from doing so. Add this behavior to the alien, and we can stop it from falling out of layout. Also, it's a good habit to make a believable space for players to be bound to. So, instead of an invisible wall, you can make an edge of a cliff or river, or something similar, depending on your game.

Jumping through platforms

Now, let's make the most fun aspect of a platformer: jumping on platforms. Here, we will make two kinds of platforms: the one that you can hit from below and the one that you can jump through from below. All platforms can be stepped on. To make the first kind of platform, we'll just simply add a Solid behavior to the objects we want to make as a platform. We'll make the boxAlt object as this kind of platform, so let's add a Solid behavior to it.

Try to test the game now, and you can see that we have made boxAlt as a solid platform. However, right now, our alien's jump isn't high enough to make it reach on top of boxAlt in one jump; let's make him jump higher. To do so, we just have to change the value of the **Jump strength** property in the Platform behavior's properties, as shown in the following screenshot:

Deceleration	1500
Jump stren...	750
Gravity	1500

Test it again, and now, our alien can jump on to the solid platform in one hop.

The next thing we want to do is make a platform that the player can jump through from below. Luckily, for us, there's also a behavior for this kind of attribute called the Jump-thru behavior. Add this to the boxEmpty object, and we have the kind of platform we want. Try jumping below the boxEmpty object, and you'll see that we have our jump-through platform set up.

There's one more thing we can do with a Jump-thru platform: to jump down while we're on top of it. Construct 2 calls this fall through, and this is an action we can add to an event. So, let's make a button press as the event. We'll make the character fall when we're holding down the down arrow key and the Space bar, because this is a pretty intuitive design that will make the code appear as follows:

| ⇒ ⌨ Keyboard | On **Space** pressed | 👾 alien | Fall 🏃 Platform down through jump-thru |
| ⌨ Keyboard | **Down arrow** is down | | |

Test the game now, and you will see that we can now fall through a Jump-thru platform.

Moving to another level

A platformer with only one level is boring; so now, we will add a new level and navigate to it. First, create a new layout, open your **Projects** bar, and right-click on the Layouts folder. Click on **Add layout** to add a new layout. A window will pop up asking you whether you want to add an event sheet to it or not. You can choose to not initially give this new layout an event sheet, but for now, we will add an event sheet along with it.

After clicking on the **Add event sheet** option, you will have a new blank layout; we'll design the second level here (it's not actually a level in a game because it's very short; I just call it that way for lack of a better word). One thing to note about designing in a new layout is that you don't have to add a new object; you can add an object from other layouts if you want to.

Remember that a new layout starts off clean; this means that it won't have the same layers as the old layouts, until you decide to add them. You can also change the new layout's size if you want to.

To do this, look at the **Projects** bar; you'll see that all the objects you've added to your project are listed under the Object types folder. To add an existing object to a new layout, drag-and-drop that object from the Object types folder to the layout. Remember that you can't drag an existing object if it is of the same type as the object that is added to the entire project; for example, a Keyboard or Touch object is already added to the entire project.

 You can add an existing object to a new layout by dragging-and-dropping it from the Object types folder to the layout.

Now that we have a new layout, design it to have the grassMid, boxAlt, and boxEmpty objects like the first layout. Before we move to the new layout in the game, we would need something that serves as a connector between the two layouts. Here, we'll use a door, add two new objects from the Tiles folder inside the Base pack folder in freebundle.zip, door_openMid, and door_openTop, and place them at the edge of the layout as follows:

The logic of changing the layout is pretty much like this: when the character collides with the door, change the location to the new layout. You can design your own logic when making your own game; for example, perhaps, the player has to press a button first. The code for our logic is as follows:

If you test your game now, you can see that we are able to go to Layout 2. However, something is strange: the player is not on Layout 2; we can't move anything on the new layout. Well, this is because we didn't put our alien object there yet, so let's add our alien object to Layout 2 as follows:

Test it, and you will see that we can now move to layer two and move our character in the new layout. However, our character doesn't play the animation; why is this happening? This is because each layout has its own event sheet, and we only animated our character in Layout 1.

All layouts have their own event sheets. If you animate an object in one layer, it won't animate in the other layers.

To make an object animate in other layers, you can copy the events that animate it. To do this, hold *Ctrl* and click on all the events you want to copy, press *Ctrl* + *C*, go to the new layout's event sheet, and press *Ctrl* + *V*. This is similar to copying and pasting in a Word document.

The event sheet for the new layout is listed in the Event sheets folder in the **Projects** bar; double-click on it to open it, and then paste the animating events there.

When copying events, be sure to click on the event, not the conditions inside the event. Copying events and copying conditions are two different things.

If you copy events, you can paste them in another event sheet or in another part of the same sheet. However, if you copy conditions, you can only paste them in another event where possible; for example, you can't put two trigger conditions in one event.

Hitting the coin box

If you still remember, we have a coin box in `layout 1` that we haven't manipulated yet. We'll modify it such that when a player hits this box from below, it will produce a coin.

This box will have an instance variable that will determine whether or not it has a coin inside. When the player collides with the box from below, we will check this instance variable. If its value is `true`, then we will spawn a coin; if it's `false`, then nothing will happen. We will also change the sprite based on this instance variable to visually indicate whether the player can hit this box or not.

So first, create an instance variable called `hasCoin` as a Boolean and change its initial value to `true`. After that, switch to the event sheet. We want to check a collision from below, so we will use the `On collision` event combined with comparing the y position of the alien with the box. If the alien's y position is bigger than the box, this means that the alien is below the box. After this, we will use a sub-event to check the Boolean instance variable's value:

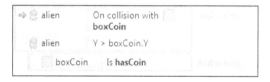

I haven't written the action yet, because here, we want to spawn an object, so let's create that object first. Insert a new sprite object and name it `coinGold`. You can get the sprite from the `Items` folder under the `Base` pack and put it somewhere off the screen. We also want to change the `boxCoin` object's sprite, so we'll add a new animation to it. Double-click on the box to open the edit image window. Add a new animation called `Disabled`, give it the image of `boxCoin_disabled` from the `Tiles` folder, and then close the edit image window.

We want this `coinGold` object to do two things when it is created: to slowly move upward and to gradually disappear. We can do these with behaviors; a Bullet behavior can be used to move upward, and to make it slower, we will just set a slower speed. To make it gradually disappear, we'll use a new behavior called Fade. A Fade behavior changes an object's opacity over time and will destroy the object by default when it is invisible. Add these two behaviors to `coinGold` and set the Bullet behavior's **Speed** property to `200` (or lower if you want). Don't forget to add a Solid behavior to `boxCoin` so that we can collide with it.

Switch to the event sheet for `layout 1`; we only need to add actions to the `boxCoin` object's `hasCoin` sub-event. We want to create a new coin here, set its angle of motion upward so that it moves up, change the animation for `boxCoin` so that the players know that it has run out of coins, and finally, we'll set the `hasCoin` instance variable to `false`.

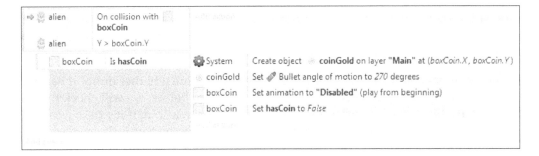

Now, we can test the game. Remember that after having more than one layout in a project, you need to be sure that the layout you selected last before testing is the layout you want to test. This is because Construct 2 always runs the layout that was opened last when testing; if you previously opened `Layout 2`, open `Layout 1` before testing. Save your project before continuing, because you'll learn something new.

Learning about physics

We will now discuss physics in Construct 2. To apply physics to an object, we only need to add a Physics behavior to it. All objects with the Physics behavior are referred to as *physics objects*. Physics is a complex subject, so I will only explain it briefly here to cover what you need to know to start experimenting with it.

If you still remember your physics class back in school, then this will be really useful here because the concepts are the same. We will create a third layout to demonstrate our physics object, so create a new layout and make it look like this:

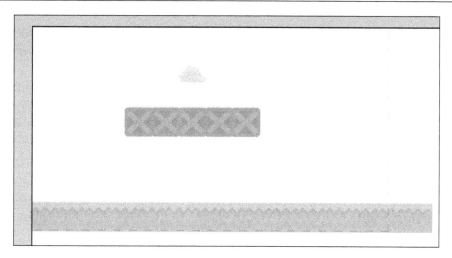

As you can see, we used two solid objects that we used to build up our levels earlier. However, we will add one new sprite object here called `rock`; the sprite for the `rock` object can be found under `Base pack\Items`. The rock doesn't do anything for now, but we'll use it as a physics object, so let's add a Physics behavior to it (the Physics behavior can be found in the movement section when you add a behavior).

 One thing to remember is that all physics objects are affected by gravity by default; this means that all physics objects will go down unless something stops them.

If we test `Layout 3`, it is expected that the rock will fall down and stop when hitting the floating platform. Unfortunately, this is not the case. The rock keeps falling down through the floating platform and the ground. Why? It's simply because physics objects only interact with other physics objects; they won't interact with objects that have Solid or Jump-thru behaviors.

Why is this? Why does Construct 2 not make the solid objects interactable with physics objects? The answer is that although the physics objects can be treated as solid objects, solid objects can't be treated as physics objects. If you still remember, Newton's third law of motion states that *every action has an equal and opposite reaction*. In our game, this means that when a physics object collides with scenery, such as our platforms, the platforms will be pushed back a bit. Solid objects won't be able to calculate this collision, so physics objects ignore them. To make our scenery interact with a physics object, we will have to make our scenery a physics object as well.

Physics objects only interact with other physics objects. To make physics objects interact with sceneries, we need to add Physics behavior to them.

But wait a minute; if we add a Physics behavior to the floating platform, then won't the platform fall as well? Did I say that all physics objects are affected by gravity? Yes, except for physics objects that are immovable. Immovable physics objects don't move at all, either by gravity or by collision from other objects; their only purpose is to act as an obstacle to other physics objects.

To make a physics object immovable, we simply need to change the value of its **Immovable** property. So now, let's add a Physics behavior to the `boxAlt` object and change its **Immovable** property to **Yes**, as shown in the following screenshot:

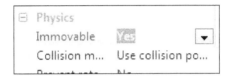

Test the game again, and the falling rock will collide with the platform as we want it to.

By now, maybe you're wondering when to use solid objects and when to use immovable physics objects. Here are the simple rules:

- If you want the players to interact with the object later in the game, use immovable physics objects. For example, you can have a box that initially can't be moved, but after the player obtains a special glove, they can move the box. In this case, you can use immovable physics objects and then set the immovable property to `No` in the code.
- If the objects only act as an obstacle, then it's better to use solid objects.
- If players can only interact with the objects in one way, then use solid objects, for example, a switch that is placed only for the player to shoot it to open a door.

Forces, impulses, torques, and joints

As we're going to use the Physics behavior, we need to get familiar with the terms in physics, especially if they're also used in Construct 2. The terms are as follows:

- **Force**: A force is an outside influence that changes an object's speed or direction. Forces are applied over time, so it's best to use forces on events that have the value of `true` for a long time, such as an `Is key down` keyboard event.

- **Impulses**: Impulses are similar to forces, but instead of being applied over time, it is a one sudden change. When you apply a force to an object, its speed and direction will change over time, but when you apply an impulse to an object, you'll change its direction in an instant. Impulses are best used on events that have the value of `true` in an instant, such as triggers.

- **Torque**: A torque is a force that's applied to rotations; it will change the speed of rotation rather than moving an object.

- **Joints**: Joints connect two objects together. They can still rotate independently, but their positions are always related to one another; if you move one object, then the joint one also moves. For example, this is used to create some kind of a device or machine that follows the rule of physics. They can be destroyed realistically.

Adding a puzzle element

Now that we know the terms used in physics, let's put them to use by adding another feature to our game: the puzzle element. Puzzles are common in platformer games; they're usually the hurdles you have to overcome in order to reach new areas to complete the level.

So, let's create a simple one for now. We'll have our character to push the rock to hit a button on the ground below; this will open a door. We'll learn how to apply a force to a physics object with the character pushing the rock. Continuing from `layout 3`, let's add a few more sprite objects to it. We'll add the obstacle door that stops us from advancing forward; you can get the sprite for it under the `Tiles` folder. After that, we'll add the button. There are two animations for it: `Default` and `Pressed`. You can get the sprites for both of them under the `Items` folder. Add a Physics behavior to both of them, set the **Immovable** property to **Yes** (do the same to the ground object), and then place them as follows:

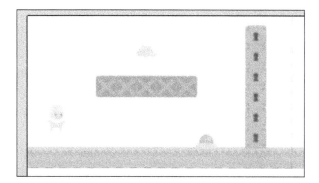

Moving our character with the Physics behavior

We also added our alien to Layout 3 to push the rock with. As with any other object in this layout, we'll add a Physics behavior to the alien, but there's one important thing to know when adding a Physics behavior to the character that the players control. When moving, physics objects don't just slide on a surface, but they'll also rotate based on a lot of things applied to them (for example, forces, impulses, and collisions with other objects). We surely don't want our character to rotate, so we'll prevent it by setting the **Prevent rotation** property to **Yes** in the **Properties** bar of `alienGreen`.

 When adding a Physics behavior to the main character, don't forget to set the **Prevent rotation** property to **Yes**, unless you want the main character to roll (for example, if the character is a ball or an armadillo).

There's another thing to keep in mind: when moving a physics object, we must only use physics actions and expressions. This is to ensure that Construct 2 does the physics calculations correctly. If we move a physics object using other behavior, such as the Platform behavior, then we might end up doing something that shouldn't be done, for example, walking through an immovable scenery object. So first, we will disable the Platform behavior by setting its property to **Disabled**.

Then, we will move the character by applying forces and impulses to it. To do so, switch over to the `layout 3` event sheet. There are three situations in which we want to move the character:

- **Moving right**: When we press the right arrow key, we will apply the force at a positive value on the *x* axis to make it move to the right

- **Moving left**: When we press the left arrow key to move to the left, we will apply the force at a negative value on the *x* axis

- **Jump**: When we jump, we will apply an impulse at a certain degree so that it moves up

The code will look as follows for the right arrow pressed event:

Similarly, for the left arrow pressed event, the code is as follows:

Finally, for the up arrow pressed event, we have the following code:

Changing the properties of the rock

By now, you can try testing the game and move around in the layout. You will find that the only object the character can interact with is the rock, because it's the only object that is not immovable. However, the rock is too easily moved; it's as if it's too light for a rock. We're going to make it harder to move.

To do so, we only need to change the value of it properties, which are friction and linear damping:

- **Friction**: This defines how easy it is for objects to move against each other while touching; it is the friction you learned back in your physics class. You can set the value between 0 and 1, with 0 being no friction at all and 1 being maximum friction.

- **Linear damping**: This is the slowdown rate of a moving object, with a value of 0 that means no slowdown at all and 1 that means maximum slowdown. Set the value of the friction and linear damping properties to 1, and we're done making the rock heavier to push.

Selecting an object via its UID

Now that everything is set and ready, we can start making the buttons react when collided with the rock, and then, we'll destroy the blue locks. The way we destroy them is not just by making them disappear with the destroy action, but we'll use impulse to throw them at an angle and then destroy them when they're outside of the layout. However, first, I want to explain what a UID is.

UIDs are unique identification numbers that are assigned to every object once they are created (you can't change them), whether in the layout or by code. No two objects have the same UID, and as these numbers are unique to each object, we can select an object by its UID. If you followed my example correctly, the UIDs for the lock objects must be between 98 and 103, but if this not the case, you can check the value of UID yourself by clicking on the object and looking at the top part of the **Properties** bar.

Object type properties	
Name	lockBlue
Plugin	Sprite
UID	103

Now, we'll use the UID in the event sheet to select the locks individually. What we want to do is when the rock collides with the button, we want change the button's animation to **Pressed** and afterwards apply an impulse to the boxes. We can just apply the same impulses to all the boxes, making them move in the same direction, but instead, we will make them move in different directions similar to an explosion effect (by picking each one of them). Remember to make the `lockBlue` objects movable, or we won't be able to move them around.

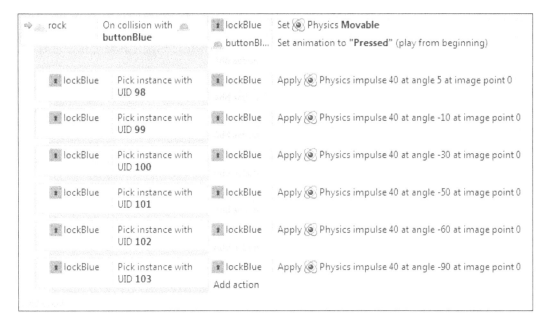

Your UID of the `lockBlue` object might be different; check them first before you write the code. We also want to destroy the locks after they're blasted or, to be more precise, we want to destroy them when they get out of the layout. Thankfully, there's a behavior for this. The behavior is simply named Destroy Outside Layout and will destroy the object if it goes outside of the layout. Add it to the `lockBlue` object.

One very important thing to do before testing your game is to check the collision polygons of your animation, especially the pressed animation of the button. If you just load the pressed button image and let Construct 2 guess the collision polygons, you would get something like this:

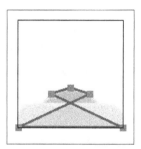

This is not good because as you can see, there are two lines that intersect each other. This can ruin the Physics behavior and give rise to a game-breaking bug, because the Physics behavior won't be able to correctly calculate the collision area of this object. To fix this, change the collision polygon to be as follows:

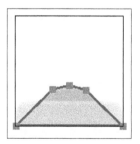

This will prevent the game-breaking bug from affecting our game and make our game run as we want it to. Test the game now and push the rock to the button; you'll see the locks being blown away. Save your project for now before you lose all the changes you made until now, and let's move on.

Joining two objects

I have given you examples of how to use forces and impulses to move physics objects around, but I haven't covered joints yet. Joints are used to join two objects together so that the distance between them is the same. We will make a bridge using joints, so, create a new layout and make it look like the one shown in the following screenshot:

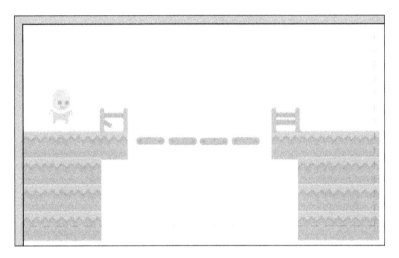

The sprites for the bridge and the fence objects are located under the `Tiles` folder. Before continuing, check the bridge's collision polygon and fix it so that no lines will intersect each other, just like the `buttonBlue` object. You want to be careful when adding physics objects, as small sprites tend to have similar collision polygons.

> Always look for collision polygons when adding an object you want to make a physics object, especially the ones with small sprites.

The fences and bridges are physics objects, but only the fences are immovable; the bridges are still movable, but we won't let them fall to the bottom. We will *tie* the bridge to the fence using joints. One thing about joints is that you can only make joints between object types, not between different instances of the same object. This is why we have a bridge object and a fence object here, because we can't just joint a bridge with another bridge.

Using joints, we join objects based on their image points; if an object doesn't have an image point, then it will be based on its origin point, which, by default, is the middle of the sprite. Now, we don't want to join the bridge by its origin point, because if you look at it, the origin point is floating above the bridge sprite. So, we will make an image point in the middle of the sprite; this will be `imagepoint 1`.

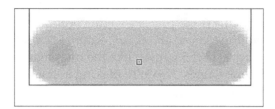

After this, we'll prevent the bridges from rotating by setting their **Prevent rotation** property to **Yes**. Switch over to the `layout 4` event sheet, and we'll join them together. You should only create joints on triggers, not on the normal events that can have the value of `true` over a long time. In our example, we'll create a joint at the start of the layout. Making a joint only needs one action, but as we have two bridges, we'll use the same action twice.

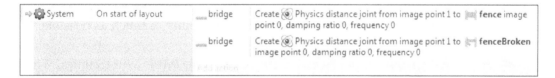

That's it! We have created a joint. Copy and paste the code to make the character move from `Layout 3` and test out this layout. You can walk on top of the bridge if you want to.

Types of physics engines in Construct 2

Construct 2 has three kinds of physics engines it uses to run physics operations:

- **box2dweb**: By default, Construct 2 uses the `box2dweb` version of the physics engine. The `box2dweb` version is based on the `box2d` physics engine; a physics engine is commonly used for native games. The `box2dweb` version is the JavaScript version of it that's intended to be used for web games.

- **box2dweb asm.js**: This is the faster version of `box2dweb`. It uses `emscripten` (a technology from Mozilla) that takes C and C++ code and produces JavaScript, creating high-performance JavaScript code as a result. This is what's called `asm.js`, and the browsers that are optimized for `asm.js` can translate this code to enable fast performance that you'd get from native C and C++ codes. However, all this happens in your browser.

- **CocoonJS native**: This is the physics engine optimized for CocoonJS wrapping. If you don't know about it, CocoonJS is a service that helps you *wrap* or *package* HTML5 games, like the ones made in Construct 2, to Android and iPhone games. If you're making a mobile game and intend to use CocoonJS to export it, it is advised that you use the CocoonJS native physics engine.

By now, maybe, some of you have a good question in mind: if the `asm.js` version of `box2dweb` is faster than normal `box2dweb` physics engine, then why not make `box2dweb asm.js` the default physics engine? It turns out that there are two drawbacks of this `asm.js` physics engine. They are as follows:

- It doesn't support the `disable collisions` action. Some old games that are created before the physics engine feature is added might use an action to disable collisions, and setting the `asm.js` as the new physics engine will break these games. To enable backward compatibility as much as possible, `asm.js` is not the default physics engine.

- In iOS native apps, it can be slower. The reason for this is a bit technical. The Safari browser on iOS has a **JIT** compiler that interprets JavaScript code and runs it. When you run native iOS apps, for example, when you wrap your game using CocoonJS or PhoneGap, JIT (Just In Time) is not supported. Note that this is still fast performance for many games. However, it's still slower than the non `asm.js` version of the same code, so if you want to deploy games for iOS, it is advised that you do not to use the `box2dweb asm.js` physics engine.

Okay, so now you know the three types of physics engine Construct 2 uses. Which one should you use? If you're deploying to mobile using CocoonJS, use the CocoonJS physics engine; if you're targeting iOS platforms, use box2dweb; and if you use the disable collisions' action in your game, use box2dweb. If you encounter anything other than these, use the `box2dweb asm.js` physics engine.

If you want to learn more about the Physics behavior, there's an online manual on Scirra's website (`https://www.scirra.com/manual/98/physics`).

Summary

Physics is a complex subject, but we delved into it in this chapter. You learned how to animate the sprite with and without looping. You also learned about three new behaviors: Platform, Scroll To, and Bound to Layout. Moreover, you learned how to create a new layout in Construct 2 and how to change to the new layout in the game. You also know the three engines that power Construct 2's physics and when they should be used. You also learned that we can pick an instance individually using UID, instead of picking all the instances at once. Finally, you also learned how to use joints in physics objects.

Our understanding of making a game in Construct 2 has increased, but so far, we have not added any competitive aspect in our game. One of the examples of a competitive element in games is a leaderboard for gamers to compete with. So, we'll make this in the next chapter.

6
Creating a
Space-shooter Game

Congratulations on reaching this chapter! By now, you have learned a lot about Construct 2 and how to use it. You now know about various behaviors and also how to use them through events. You have also learned about expressions and sub-events that are useful when making more complex games. However, there's still one thing missing if you want to create an engaging experience: competition.

Making players compete with their friends is a good way to improve the gameplay experience. One way to do this is to add a leaderboard to your game so that players will fight for the position of the highest score. We will add this element to a space-shooter game. In creating this space-shooter game, you will learn how to create a scrolling background and spawn a new object related to an existing object.

In this chapter, you will learn:

- How to create a scrolling background
- How to store variables in Construct 2 and compare them with other stored values
- How Construct 2 stores data on a player's computer or device

Setting the stage

So, just like the previous chapter, we'll start by designing our layout. The sprites used in this chapter can be found under the Space shooter folder under Sprites in freebundle.zip. However, we want to change the default resolution first, because our space shooter will be a vertical one and not horizontal. If you start with a new empty project, then, by default, you'll get a resolution of 854 x 480. To change this, we will simply change the value of the window size in **Project Properties**. To open the project properties, click on the **View** link in **Project Properties** or click on the project name, which is the first item in the **Project** bar on the right-hand side.

Clicking on this will show the project properties with a lot of configurations that you can apply to your project, such as changing the name and description of the game, choosing what preview browser to use, and selecting the physics engine for the physics behavior, among other things. For now, let's change the window size to 480 x 854. This is the WFVGA resolution, which is a display resolution of 854 x 480, and is approximately the 16:9 display ratio of the widescreen video. This is considered a *safe* resolution that doesn't crop any of the images. I swapped the width and the height to make it a portrait mode instead of landscape.

Preview effects	Yes
Window Size	**480, 854**
Configuration Settings	
Preview browser	(default)

As you can see in the layout, changing this property also changes the dotted lines that form our game window to a more vertical shape. After that, add a new background and a `playerShip` object. To make the player move, give it the 8 Direction behavior, and we'll also prevent him from moving off the screen with the Bound to Layout behavior. Don't forget to set the 8 Direction behavior's **Set angle** property to No because we want it to face upward at all times.

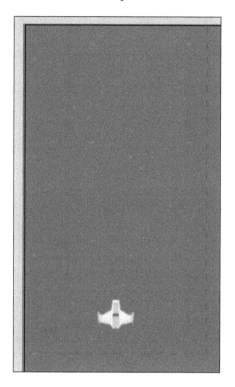

Scrolling the stage

Now, just like any other space-shooter game, we will make the player go forward to the enemy base and destroy all the enemy ships that get in his way. However, actually, the screen doesn't scroll anywhere. The player's ship moving forward is just an illusion; it is the stage that moves backward and makes it look like the player's ship is advancing forward. This is a trick commonly used in game development to make the player move forward. You can either move it forward or move everything else back, and you'll achieve the same result.

So now, create a new layer called **Stars** and add it below the **Main** layer but above the **Background** layer. We created our ship in the **Main** layer, and we will also create enemies in the same layer. The **Stars** layer is where we will create the stars that will move backward, or downward in this case, to create the illusion of the player moving forward. To do this, first create a star sprite object and add it in the **Stars** layer, and then give a Bullet behavior to it so that it can move. You can use the star sprites present in `Sprites\Space shooter\Effects`. Then, switch over to the event sheet, because we're going to move the stars down using code.

The logic is like this: every half second, we'll create a new star at a random position on the screen, and then, we'll change its angle of movement so that it moves down. We'll also change its speed so that the stars don't move too fast. Translate it into code, and you will get the following result:

If you test the game now, you can see the stars going to the bottom of the screen, creating an illusion of the player moving forward. If, while testing, you move the ship too far to the right-hand side or to the bottom of the screen, you'll realize that the player ship can still go out of the window, while it can't go past the top and the left-hand side of the screen.

What caused this? Didn't we already add the Bound to Layout behavior? Well, it's because we bound it to the game layout, not to the game window. To bind the ship to the window, we'll have to resize the layout to fit the game window. We can easily set this from the layout properties; we need to change the size of the layout to be the same as that of the window.

Now, the player is totally bound to the window.

Creating the enemy

Next up, we're going to make the enemy, because a space shooter isn't fun without something to shoot at. Add a new sprite object called `enemy` and place it on the **Main** layer. The enemy will do two things: moving and shooting. Moving our enemy object is easy, and it is the same as moving the stars. So, follow those steps again. Now, I'm going to explain how to make the enemy randomly.

We'll create the enemy at a random position every 2 seconds, and after that, the enemy will move slowly downward. So, let's first add a Bullet behavior to our enemy object and change the set angle value to `No`. Then, we'll change the speed to `100` to make it move slowly. Next, we'll create the enemy at a random *x* position onscreen and set the angle of motion to `90` as follows:

Test the game now, and you'll see that we have created the enemies randomly. Next, we'll tell them to shoot.

The word **shooting** actually means that the enemy will create a new object relative to itself, and the newly created object will move on its own. In this case, we will create a new bullet and shoot it downwards. To do this, we'll have to create two things:

- The bullet object
- An imagepoint on the enemy

So, let's add a new sprite object as the bullet. We'll name this bullet `enemyBullet` to differentiate it from the player's bullet. Before finally adding this bullet by closing the edit image window, we'll rotate this sprite 90 degrees clockwise. The reason we do this is because this object will use the Bullet behavior for movement, and we want to be able to change its angle according to the Bullet behavior's angle of motion. The zero degrees angle of motion refers to the right-hand side of the screen; rotating the sprite will make it easier if you want the enemies to be able to fire in more directions than just one.

Close the edit image window to add the bullet to the layout and put it somewhere off the screen. Another thing we want to do is destroy the bullet automatically after it goes out of the layout, because there's no point in keeping a bullet that we no longer use. We can do this using code, but there's also a behavior for this called Destroy Outside Layout; this will destroy the object when it gets out of the layout. Add this behavior to `enemyBullet`.

Next, we'll add an imagepoint to the enemy object. This imagepoint will be the point where the bullet is created or spawned by the enemy. Position the imagepoint in the lower part of the middle half of the sprite. We'll also need to make the enemy shoot the bullet at some interval of time instead of at every tick. So, we'll add a Timer behavior to our enemy object.

The logic to make the enemy shoot is this: when the enemy is created, we'll start the timer to set the interval for each shot and make this timer repeatable. Every time the timer is *fired*, we will spawn a new bullet at the imagepoint that we created. After that, we'll change the angle of motion for the bullet to make it go downward. So, the code is as follows for the `enemy On created` event:

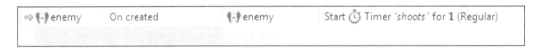

The following is the code for the `enemy On timer "shoots"` event:

This will make the enemy shoot every second. If you think the interval is too short, you can change the time the timer is fired at. Test the game now, and you'll see that we have created our enemies successfully.

Test the game now, and you'll see that we have created our enemies successfully.

Deleting offscreen objects

By now, we have two objects that always go offscreen and are never used again: the enemy and the star. It's a good habit to destroy offscreen objects that are no longer needed, so now, we'll delete them.

We'll destroy the enemy objects when they go more than 100 pixels off the bottom of the screen, and we'll destroy the star objects when they are more than 50 pixels from the bottom of the screen. There's a system's expression called `LayoutHeight` that tells us the height of the current layout, and we'll use this to compare the *y* position of both objects. Look at the following two events:

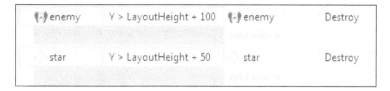

Making the player shoot at enemies

It's good to have the enemies shoot at us, but without the ability to fight back, the players won't find the game fun; so let's make our player shoot at the enemies. We'll make it a little different than enemy shots; for the player, we'll make it such that the player shoots when they are pressing a key on the keyboard, for example, the Z key.

To do this, we surely need to add a Keyboard object to our project. Then, we'll give a Timer behavior to the `playerShip` object. After that, we'll add a player bullet object to the layout and add the Bullet behavior to it. Just like the `enemyBullet` object, we'll also rotate this object 90 degrees clockwise. Finally, we'll add a new imagepoint for `playerShip` to be the place where the bullet is spawned. After that, our preparation is set.

Now, let's design the logic for player shooting. We will start the timer when the player presses the Z key; we will only check for when the player first presses Z, because we don't want to start the timer at every tick that the Z key is pressed. We will stop the timer when the player releases the Z key; this is to make the shooting stop. The shooting takes place when the timer is fired, and we'll set the timer to fire every half a second. If we write this using code, it will be as follows:

⇨ Keyboard	On Z pressed	playerShip	Start Timer 'shoots' for **0.5** (Regular)
⇨ Keyboard	On Z released	playerShip	Stop Timer 'shoots'
⇨ playerShip	On Timer 'shoots'	playerShip	Spawn **playerBullet** on layer "Main" *(image point 1)*
		playerBullet	Set Bullet angle of motion to *270* degrees

Test the game now, and you will see that the player can now shoot when the Z key is being held down and stops shooting when we no longer press it. Maybe you're asking, "Why don't we use the Keyboard object's is key down event to check for when the Z key is being pressed and spawn a new bullet if it's true? Isn't it the same?" Well, it isn't. If we use the is key down event, this event will be true for every tick, and the player's ship will shoot bullets at every tick. This is something we don't want and is something that's hard to control. Using a combination of a Timer behavior and the On key pressed trigger makes it easier to change the interval of the player's shots.

Adding the particle effects

So, now that both the enemies and the player are able to shoot, let's make the bullets hit them instead of passing through them. To make it look like it's a hit, we'll simply destroy the bullets when they collide with their target. So, we'll destroy the player's bullets when they collide with the enemy, and we'll destroy the enemy's bullets when they collide with the player. However, only making them disappear won't feel right for the player when they play the game; so, let's add two more sprite objects to be shown when the bullet collides and name them playerBlast and enemyBlast. Then, let's add the code to show them all:

The code for the On collision with enemy event is as follows:

Test your game, and you can see explosion effects appear on impact with the enemy:

This seems good, but the explosion effects don't disappear after being called. Let's add a Fade behavior to both `playerBlast` and `enemyBlast` objects to make them automatically fade until destroyed. The Fade behavior will make the object gradually disappear until it vanishes; the duration for it can be changed from its properties. After that, this behavior can destroy the object after fading out.

Storing data in Construct 2

This is usually the time when I teach you to destroy the enemies and add scores to the game. However, because the focus of this chapter is to store data from the game, we'll cover this first. There are four objects we can use to store data in Construct 2: array, dictionary, WebStorage, and XML. We're not going to cover XML in this book, because XML is a bit hard for beginners of programming, but only knowing the first three is enough for you to save data from your game.

Getting to know arrays

An array, in programming context, is a list of ordered things. An array can be a list of all text values, all number values, or a combination of text and numbers. In programming languages, arrays are written as a list of data inside a square bracket; so, in this book, I will also write an array in such a way. For example, an array of countries will be `["Canada", "USA", "Russia", "Italy", "Germany", "England"]`, while an array of numeric values will be `[100, 250, 350, 150, 600, 450]`.

One thing to keep in mind when dealing with arrays is that arrays are zero-based indexed lists, which means that they start with 0 instead of 1. So, in the earlier country list, `"Canada"` is array member zero, and `"Italy"` is member number three. Remember this because this is a mistake beginners often make.

Understanding the elements of an array

By default, Construct 2's array contains 10 empty members. Members are elements or values that are stored in an array. Taking our countries array as an example, we can say that the members of the array are as follows:

```
countries[0] = "Canada"
countries[1] = "USA"
countries[2] = "Russia"
```

```
countries[3] = "Italy"
countries[4] = "Germany"
countries[5] = "England"
countries[6] = empty
countries[7] = empty
countries[8] = empty
countries[9] = empty
```

When you want to add another member to the array, you have to add it between the ranges of the total number of elements (I'll explain this later in the *Using arrays in your game* section). So, you can only add to countries[6] through countries[9]; trying to add an element to countries[11], for example, doesn't do anything. It doesn't change the array at all. If you want to add more members than the total number of elements of the array, you must first change its length.

A length is the total number of elements the array can hold. An array of 10 members means that the array has a length of 10. To add the eleventh or twelfth members to an array, we must first change its length.

 Arrays can only contain a set number of data (it's 10 by default) called a length. Arrays don't automatically increase their length; it must be done manually. You can only add new members to the array if it is within its length.

To change the length of an array, we only need to change its value in the **Properties** bar. In the following screenshot, **Width** is the length of the *x* axis of an array, **Height** is the length of the *y* axis, and **Depth** is the *z* axis. More about these axes will be explained in the next section.

Properties	
Width	10
Height	1
Depth	1

One-dimensional and multidimensional arrays

What I'm about to cover here is a little difficult, but since this is a feature of an array and the array object in Construct 2 supports it, I have to teach you about it. This is for advanced readers; you can skip this part if you want to. There are two kinds of arrays:

- **One-dimensional arrays**: These are arrays that only contain one-dimensional data on the x axis. An example of a one-dimensional array is the list of countries and numerical values that I mentioned earlier.

- **Multidimensional arrays**: These are arrays that contain data in more than one dimension. A two-dimensional array can be imagined as a table where the data is stored in its x and y axes.

  An example of this is a table that contains the stats of every enemy, which looks as follows:

	Basic enemy	Defender unit	Striker unit
Health	50	50	30
Attack power	10	10	5
Defense	0	20	10
Speed	5	2	20
Bonus score	10	20	35

The other multidimensional array is a three-dimensional array where data is stored in the x, y, and z axes. This can be seen when you store data in a cube-shaped storage. In general, you probably don't need to use a multidimensional array in your game. For simple games, a one-dimensional array is enough to store player data.

Storing data in a dictionary

A dictionary is pretty similar to an array; this means that it can also store text and numerical values. However, there are two differences in a dictionary: it doesn't order its members, and it stores values associated with keys. An array has the first member stored in index number 0; it also has a second and third member stored in index numbers 1 and 2, respectively, and so on. A dictionary doesn't have ordering like this.

A dictionary stores its values associated with keys. Keys are strings of text used to access a value. So, for example, we store a value of Joe with the username key, and a value of 250 with the scores key. Retrieving the username key will give us Joe, and retrieving scores will give us 250. Remember that keys are case sensitive, so username and UserName store two different values.

Comparison between arrays and dictionaries

Now, you know that arrays and dictionaries are pretty similar, with a few differences as follows:

Arrays	Dictionaries
The positions of the members are ordered	The members have no ordering; they are associated with a key
To retrieve a member's value, we will use its index position	To retrieve a member's value, we will use the key that's associated with the value we want to retrieve
Can be sorted	Can't be sorted
Allows complex data storage with multidimensional arrays	Allows only simple storage with keys

Noting these differences, there are situations where we use arrays and where we use dictionaries. We will use arrays when we:

- Want to be able to sort the data, whether ascending or descending
- Want to retrieve the value by some mathematical rules; for example, we might want to see members 1 to 5 and not all
- Store complex data using multidimensional arrays

We'll use dictionaries when we:

- Want to create a list of values we can associate with a name.
- Want to retrieve a value based on text; for example, we can create an upgradePoints dictionary and store a value with a Hero1 key. When we want to get the upgrade points for Hero1, we can just call the dictionary with the Hero1 key.

These are just examples; you can find your own uses based on your creativity.

Using arrays in your game

Alright, I have explained a lot about arrays and dictionaries; now is the time to put them to use. First of all, let's create a global variable named scores with type number; we'll use this to store our scores. After this, let's add an array object to the game project; array objects will be added to the whole project. Name this object scoreArray.

We'll increase the `scores` variable by 10 every time an enemy ship is destroyed; we'll destroy an enemy ship every time it is hit by the player's lasers. Usually, in other shooter games, the enemies will have health that decreases until they're destroyed, but in our case, we'll destroy our enemies with one shot. So, we'll edit the event where `playerBullet` hits an enemy, and then, we'll add one more event when the enemy is destroyed.

We have added a value to the `scores` global variable, but we haven't added it to our array yet. There are two ways of adding an element to an array:

- **Pushing it**: Push is the usual command in traditional programming languages when you want to insert an element to an array. There are two kinds of pushes: push back or push front. Push back is inserting an element to the last index of an array; for example, if an array of 10 empty elements is *pushed back*, then the new member is on index 9. If it is *pushed back* again, then the first element is on index 8, the new element is on index 9, and so on. Push front is the same as push back, but the new element is pushed to the first index of an array.

- **Setting the value at a location**: Setting the value at a location is easiest to understand, because it doesn't change the position of another member of the array unless it's at the same position. So, using the countries array that we saw earlier, we know that index numbers 6 to 9 are empty. Adding `China` to index number 7 doesn't change the position of other elements; it simply adds a new value. The only important thing to remember here is that it will erase the old value if the index position specified already has a value. So, for example, if we insert `Japan` to index 2 in our pervious countries example, it will erase `Russia` and replace it with `Japan`.

We'll let players collect as many scores as they can before we store the scores to our array. We'll do this when the player is destroyed, so let's edit the event where the enemies' bullets hit the player and add another event for when the player is destroyed:

The code for the `On destroyed` event is as follows:

This will set the value of `scoreArray` at index 0 to the `scores` variable. When setting the value, you might see that there are `set at XY` and `set at XYZ` actions. We will use `set at X`. The other two are used when you insert a value to a multidimensional array that I explained earlier.

Inserting data into a dictionary

Now, let's try to do the same thing with a dictionary. First, we will add a dictionary object to our game. Just like an array, a dictionary is added to the whole project. Add a new dictionary object to our game and call it `scoreDictionary`.

Usually in a game, you use either an array or a dictionary, and not both, but we already have an event here that uses an array. We can just delete it before adding our code snippets for when we use a dictionary, but here, I'll show you how to disable code. First, select the event that you want to disable; for us, this will be the event where the player's ship is destroyed, and we will set a value to an array. After that, press the *D* key, and the event(s) and action(s) will be disabled, or you can right-click and select **Toggle Disabled**. Disabled events and actions are marked with a strikethrough over their text, as shown in the following screenshot:

There is more than one way to disable an event:

- You can disable an event by selecting it and pressing the *D* key
- You can disable multiple events at once by selecting the ones you want to disable and pressing the *D* key
- You can disable one or more actions in an event without disabling the event
- Selecting a disabled event/action and pressing the *D* key will re-enable that event/action

Now, let's add our code to add a new member to the dictionary. When adding a new value inside a dictionary, we will define the key along with it. We're storing the user's score here, so we'll simply call the key `score`:

Retrieving the value in an array and dictionary

We now know how to store data to our array and dictionary, but what good is storing data without knowing how to retrieve it? I'll show you how to do this with both objects. Before that, we'll create a place for them on the screen. Let's create two text objects: one is called `arrayScoreText`, and the other is `dictionaryScoreText`; place them in the upper-left corner of the screen as follows:

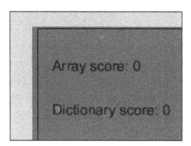

Then, in the event sheet, we will add actions to show their values in the respective text objects. For this, we will use two On player destroyed events: one to retrieve the array's value and another to retrieve the dictionary's value. To retrieve the array's value, we will use an expression that gives us the value of the array's member, based on the index number we supply to it. This expression is called an At() expression, and we will supply the index number between its brackets. We'll add the value we get from it to the text object:

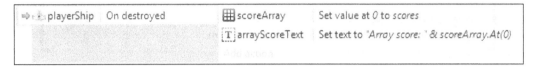

Next, we'll retrieve the value from the dictionary. To do so, we need help from an expression, but instead of an index number, this expression needs (or takes) the key of the value we want to retrieve. We'll add the returned value to the appropriate text object:

Test the game now, and you will see that the game shows the score the players get after they die.

Storing data in the player's machine

We know how to store data in an array and dictionary and how to show them onscreen, great! However, there's one thing to keep in mind when working with arrays and dictionaries: they will lose their values when the game is closed. The players might close the web browser window. Whenever they do this, they close the game, and the game will not remember the last value you put inside the array or the dictionary.

In most cases, this is not what we want. If we want to keep a score and then compare it to create a leaderboard, we want the game to remember it even after the game is closed. To do this, we need to store the data in the player's computer. So, when we start the game next time, our game can still remember the player's score. How do we do this? Using a WebStorage object.

A WebStorage object does not store data in an online storage despite the name. It stores data on the player's computer locally. It also works when used to create offline games with node-webkit and mobile wrappers such as CocoonJS (I'll explain these when it comes to exporting your game).

WebStorage does not store data in the browser cache, so if the user wants to clear the browser cache, their data is not lost. However, the WebStorage data will be lost if they clear the cookies or offline website data. However, on platforms that are not web browsers with an address bar (the Windows 8 app), there's no way for players to delete the WebStorage data.

Remember that the WebStorage object associates data with the domain. For example, all games that are hosted on myGamesSites.com share the same data, but games hosted on facebook.com have different data and can't access data from myGamesSites.com.

There are two places where a WebStorage object stores data:

- **Local storage**: This is permanent; the data is not gone until the player clears their cache
- **Session storage**: This lasts as long as the current browser session; if the session ends, the data is deleted

Using WebStorage to store data

Now, let's use the WebStorage object to store our data. Insert WebStorage into your project; we'll add the scores value to WebStorage when the player is destroyed, just like the array and dictionary. So, first disable the two events that add a new value to the array and dictionary object, and we'll create a new playerShip On destroyed event to insert new data to WebStorage. The way to add a new value to WebStorage is the same as the way in which we added a dictionary, where it associates a key to a value. So let's create a playerScore key to store the scores, like this:

This is easy enough, but in order to make a leaderboard, we need to show not only the scores from the latest play session, but also from the previous ones. We will later show all this data to the player by making a leaderboard table. So, for example, if we have 5 game sessions, we want the data in WebStorage to be like this (the left part is the key, and the right part is the value):

```
"playerScore1": 50
"playerScore2": 100
"playerScore3": 70
"playerScore4": 20
"playerScore5": 60
```

The players might play for more than five game sessions, and we want our code to be able to handle this kind of situation. If we use the previous code, the value of the playerScore key of our WebStorage object will be changed every time the player dies, because storing another value to a key that already exists will overwrite it. So, what should we do?

First, we'll create a new key on the WebStorage object; let's call it gameSession to make it clear that this key will record how many game sessions have been played. We'll create it every time the layout starts to mark the beginning of a new game session. There's a special thing when we create this key; we'll only create it if it isn't created earlier. This way, we won't overwrite the last value of the gameSession key. We do this using the is local key exists action of our WebStorage object and then invert the condition.

After that, let's make a new global variable to add the gameSession number to the key when we save the value to WebStorage; we'll call this variable sessionNumber and make it a string. Why a string; isn't the value that is stored to the gameSession key a number? Well, it's because unlike a dictionary where you can retrieve text or numbers, all the values you retrieve from WebStorage are always text.

You can change the type of a value from text to a number using a system expression, int(). The int() expression is short for integer, which is a round number data type in traditional programming languages.

Now, we have what we need to make our code remember several game sessions, so let's do this. However, first, delete the action when we set the playerScore local key to our WebStorage object, because we're going to replace this with a different set of code snippets. When the player is destroyed, we want to retrieve the gameSession key and store the value in our sessionNumber global variable. We can retrieve a value using a localValue() expression and passing the key to it:

After that, we will increment the gameSession value by one and store it back to WebStorage so that we can store the score for the upcoming game sessions. We will do this by changing the sessionNumber variable to a number, incrementing it by one, and storing it to WebStorage.

The previous code does not change the value of the sessionNumber variable; we only use its value to change the gameSession key. Now, we'll store the score to WebStorage using a key with a sessionNumber variable added at the end.

Making the leaderboard

The game now stores different scores for different game sessions, and that's great! What is left now is to actually show them in a leaderboard. So now, create a new layout where we'll create the leaderboard and give it the same background as the first layout. We'll add two text objects that we'll use for the leaderboard on this layout; name them `highscoreNameText` and `highscoreText` to show the key and the score, respectively, in the leaderboard.

At the start of the layout, we'll look at the `WebStorage` object and see how many elements it has. For each element, we'll create new text objects to show the key and the score to the screen. Here, we're using another concept in programming that I haven't explained yet: `loop`.

Understanding looping

What is looping? I explained in *Chapter 1, Downloading and Understanding Construct 2*, that the code in Construct 2, like in any other language, is executed from top to bottom. So, the code in Construct 2 is run from the first event to the last event without stopping, that is, unless it encounters a loop.

A loop is a block of code that is always executed as long as its conditions are still true. At the end of a loop block, the program will check whether the conditions have been met or not. If not, the execution starts again from the beginning of the loop; if the conditions have been met, the loop ends, and the execution continues to the next code.

I'm sure it's going to be easier to understand when we put this knowledge into practice. We'll do this using one kind of loop: a `for` loop. A `for` loop is a loop that goes on for a specified number of time; this is specified by its start and end indexes. What we want to do is loop for the total count of members of our `WebStorage` object, and then, we will create the two texts to show our leaderboard. A `for` loop is used when we know exactly how many times to loop; in this instance, we're looping for the total count of members of our `WebStorage` object.

Using a loop in our leaderboard

There are three things we need for a `for` loop:

- **The name of the loop**: This is used to identify the loop in case there is more than one loop in your code. It can be an empty text.
- **The start index**: This is the starting index of the loop.
- **The end index**: This is the ending index of the loop.

The `for` loop will increment the loop index by one at the end of the loop and then start the code from the top again. The loop ends when the loop index has reached the end index.

We'll use two `WebStorage` expressions in this loop: `localAt` and `localKeyAt`. The `localAt` expression is used to retrieve the value at an index; we can retrieve the value stored in `WebStorage` by its index number or by the key. Just like an array, `WebStorage` is a zero-based index, so the first member is at index 0, the second one is at index 1, and so on. A `localKeyAt` expression will give us the key at a certain index.

 There are two ways to retrieve a value from `WebStorage`: by its index position using the `localKeyAt` expression or by its key using the `localValue` expression.

Remember that at the beginning of `Layout 1`, we created a key called `gameSession` in our `WebStorage` object. This key will be at index 0, and our `playerScore` set of keys will be at index 1, 2, 3, and so on. So, our `for` loop will loop from index 1 to the end of `WebStorage`.

To define *end of WebStorage*, we will count the number of local keys stored in `WebStorage` and deduct it by one. Why do we deduct it? Because `WebStorage` is a zero-based index, but if we count it, we will get the total number of local keys stored, which is not a zero-based index. We will name our loop `leaderboard` and use the following code along with it:

Then, we will create the two text strings and put them in the appropriate places. We want the *y* position of the text strings to increase every time the loop index increases so that the position of the new text is below the last one. After that, we'll change the value of the text strings. One will show the key; we will do this using a `WebStorage` expression, `localKeyAt`, and we'll supply the loop index to get the key at an index. The other text will show the score; we will do this with the `localAt` expression that will give us the value that's stored in an index.

We are now ready to test our leaderboard, but first, we must make the game switch to `Layout 2` after the player is destroyed. So, let's go back to the event sheet in `Layout 1` and add two more actions. The first one will wait for 1 second before changing the layout, and the second action will change the layout.

Now, test your game. Make sure that you're testing from `Layout 1` and not `Layout 2`. After the player ship is destroyed, the game will take you to the second layout where you can see a leaderboard similar to the one shown in the following screenshot:

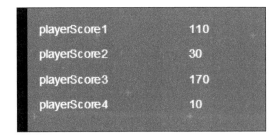

Congratulations! You have made your own basic leaderboard. Other games that use leaderboards also follow similar techniques but use online storage instead of local data like us.

Summary

You learned a lot of different things in this chapter, from changing the size of the game window and layout to using an imagepoint to spawn a new object relative to an existing object. You then learned about different objects to store data: arrays, dictionaries, and `WebStorage`. You also learned how to store data in an array and dictionary.

You then learned in a bit more detail about the differences between an array and a dictionary and when to use them. Another small but useful thing that you learned is how to disable and re-enable events. After that, we found out how we can store data on the player's computer instead of saving it only in the game. After that, we retrieved this data in the later playing sessions. Finally, we discovered a concept called `loop`, which can be used to create a leaderboard.

If you want to delve deeper into the complicated topics I covered here, you can visit some of the pages at Scirra's online manual; for example:

- Arrays: `https://www.scirra.com/manual/108/array`
- Dictionaries: `https://www.scirra.com/manual/140/dictionary`
- WebStorage: `https://www.scirra.com/manual/120/webstorage`

That's a lot of stuff covered this time around; I hope you understood all of it. You learned about a lot of things Construct 2 can do for you, but there's still one more thing you can do with the tool: create smarter enemies. In the next chapter, we will make our enemies capable of telling where the player is and acting accordingly.

7
Making a Battle Tank Game

You have learned a lot up until now. The last thing we covered was how to store multiple values in an array or dictionary and how to access them. You also learned about WebStorage that will store data in the player's computer; this data can be accessed when the game is played at a later time.

However, now we will develop on what we know so far. I will show you more ways in which we can use arrays other than to store the player's score. We'll also create a new kind of enemy. Earlier, our enemies were really simple and easy to make; they just went down and shot straight down. Now, we'll give our enemies a little AI to make them cleverer, by making a battle tank game.

In this chapter, you will learn how to:

- Combine an array with the gameplay mechanic
- Group objects in a group
- Create a turret that can detect nearby enemies
- Play music and sound effects in the game
- Make simple AI for enemies

Setting up the layout

As always, we'll begin by creating the layout for our game. Unfortunately, for us, there is no sprite in `freebundle.zip` that fits a battle tank game. However, we can use two sprites to make a tank: one sprite for the base of the tank and another one for the turret.

First, add two sprite objects to the layout and name them `tankTurret` and `tankBase`. The `tankBase` sprite is from `UI elements\Adventure pack`. Pick any square icon; in this example, I will use the `buttonSquare_blue_pressed` image. For the turret, pick an arrow image that points to the right, such as `arrowSilver_right`. If you place these images on top of each other, you will see an icon similar to the one shown in the following screenshot:

This looks good enough for a tank. However, for it to be called a tank, the base and the turret must act like one, that is, if one is created, so is the other, and if one is destroyed, so is the other. How do we do this? Well, Construct 2 has a feature called **container** to group objects together.

Using a container

So, what is a container? A container is a feature in Construct 2 that eases the creation of an object composed of more than one object. Sometimes, when making a game, you'll have an object that is too complex to be represented in one object. Using a container, we can treat multiple objects as if they are one. In our example here, we have a tank that consists of two sprites: the base and the turret. Adding these two to a container enables them to rotate and move independently; they also have their own instance variables. This is useful, for example, when you want to create a side-scrolling game in which you can make the hand and sword check against collision with a target enemy to hurt them and the player's body to be checked against collision with the enemy's attack.

All objects in a container have the following traits:

- If one object in a container is created, all the other objects in the same container would also be created
- If one object in a container is destroyed, all other objects in the same container would also be destroyed
- If an event manipulates one object in a container, all other objects in the same container would also be manipulated

These traits are made because Construct 2 treats a container as one object.

Now, let's create a container. To do so, select one of the objects you want in the container, such as the `tankTurret` object. After that, you can see the **Container** section of its property in the **Properties** bar. If it doesn't have any container yet, it will say **No container** along with a blue **Create** link beside it; click on the link to create the container.

Construct 2 will open a new window to select objects to add to this container. For now, we only have the `tankBase` object; so let's add this, click on it, and press the **OK** button. The `tankBase` object is now added to the container; if you look at the **Properties** bar, you'll see it. Click on the two objects alternately and look at the **Properties** bar. You can see that they are added to each other's container.

You can add another object to that container or remove an existing member from it. Now, every time a `tankBase` object is created, Construct 2 will also create a `tankTurret` object. However, it is not enough to have them created at the same time; we want the turret to stick to the base so that when the base tank moves, the turrets follow.

Pinning an object to another object

We can pin an object to another object using a behavior called Pin; this behavior will pin an object to another, making it maintain its distance and angle with the object it's pinned to. As we will mainly move `tankBase` and make `tankTurret` follow it, we will add this behavior to the `tankTurret` object.

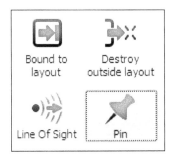

After adding the Pin behavior, we will use it to pin to another object, in this case, the `tankBase` object. This pinning is done by code, and we will pin the `tankTurret` object when the turret is created. The turret is created when the base is created, so we'll pin the turret when the base is created. While pinning, we have to decide whether to pin by position only, or angle only, or both.

> Pinning by its position will make the pinned object retain its position relative to the other object, but when the other object rotates, the pinned object doesn't change its angle.
>
> Pinning by its angle will make the pinned object retain its angle relative to the other object, but it doesn't change its position when the other object moves.
>
> Pinning by both angle and position will make the pinned object retain its position and angle relative to the other object.

For now, we want to pin by both position and angle, so the code is as follows:

Moving the units

We have grouped two objects in a container; now, let's make them move. To move the units, we will first select them and then click on a place on the game to move the selected units there. We need an instance variable to make the units know whether or not they've been selected. This instance variable is a Boolean variable; let's call it `selected`, and we'll create it in the `tankBase` object.

To be able to select a unit, the game must respond to a mouse input; so we'll add a Mouse object in our project. Then, we have to move the unit, but how do we do this? Construct 2 has a simple way to move an object with a Pathfinding behavior. This behavior takes a position to move to and then moves the object to this position. Sounds simple enough, so let's add this behavior to the `tankBase` object.

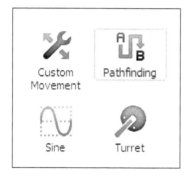

Now that we have this behavior, we can start moving our units. There is a way to move them: players must first click on the unit they want to move to select them; we marked the selected units by changing their selected instance variable to `true`:

After that, the players must click on a place in the game they want the selected units to move to, and we'll tell the units to find a way there using a Pathfinding behavior:

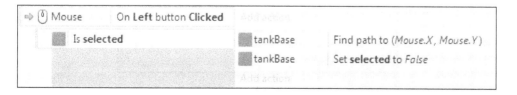

If the units can find a way there, they will go there:

We have made our selected units go where we want them to! Test the game now and you will see the units moving to where you click with the mouse. They even rotate nicely when changing directions.

Adding obstacles

I think a blank white background is pretty boring for a level, don't you? So, let's add a few obstacles in the way of our unit. We will place these obstacles in their own layer, so create a new layer called **Obstacles** and put it between the **Main** and **Background** layers.

We will use a tiled background to make the obstacles so that we can create several kinds of obstacles. Unfortunately, there isn't a sprite in the Sprites folder with a size of 16 x 16 or 32 x 32 that we can use for this, so we'll have to make our own. First, we'll create a tiled background object and name it tiledObstacle, and then, in the edit image window, we'll resize it by clicking on the Resize icon.

Now, change the value to 32 x 32.

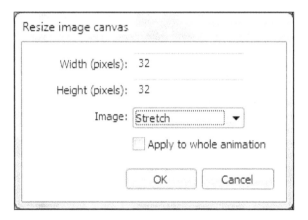

After we resize it, we'll color the image in the orange color. Close the edit image window and place the tiled obstacles in three ways: vertically, horizontally, and diagonally, as shown in the following screenshot:

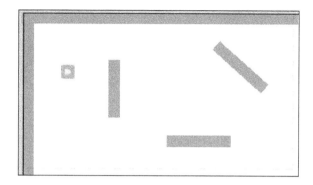

We've got three kinds of obstacles; this is a good way to show you how the Pathfinding behavior works. If you test the game now, our unit can still walk through the obstacles. Why? This is because the Pathfinding behavior doesn't see them as obstacles.

There are two ways for the Pathfinding behavior to recognize obstacles: solid and custom. By default, the Pathfinding behavior sees solid objects as obstacles and will try to move around them. The other setting, **Custom**, means that we have to tell the Pathfinding behavior which objects are the obstacles. Remember that solid objects are objects with a Solid behavior, which makes them impassable by other objects. You can change the setting in the **Properties** bar.

For now, let me show you how to use solid objects as obstacles. We only need to add a solid behavior to the tiledObstacle objects, and the Pathfinding behavior already knows that they are obstacles. Test the game after you've added a Solid behavior to the obstacles, and you can see that our unit now tries to evade them.

Making custom obstacles for the units

Alright, we know how simple it is to make obstacles with solid objects, but how do we make custom obstacles that aren't solid objects? To answer this, we will first create another object to be this custom obstacle. Add another sprite object to the layout, and as we don't have the appropriate sprite for this, let's resize it to 32 x 32 and give it a blue color. Name this sprite `civilians`; it'd make sense for tanks to avoid them. We will create custom obstacles when we want one object with the Pathfinding behavior to evade an obstacle, and when we also want the other object to not evade the same obstacle.

We'll then change the **Obstacles** property to **Custom** so that the Pathfinding behavior will look for custom objects as obstacles.

So, how do we tell the Pathfinding behavior which objects are the obstacles? We will do this using code. When `tankBase` is created, we'll tell it which objects are the obstacles using the `add obstacle` action. We'll add the `civilians` and `tiledObstacle` objects as obstacles; we want to add the solid objects in this way because the Pathfinding behavior's property has been changed to **Custom**. So, on the event sheet, edit the `tankBase` property's `On created` action to be as follows:

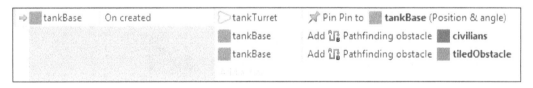

After this, place the civilians objects somewhere so that it would hinder the tank's movement. This is represented in the following screenshot:

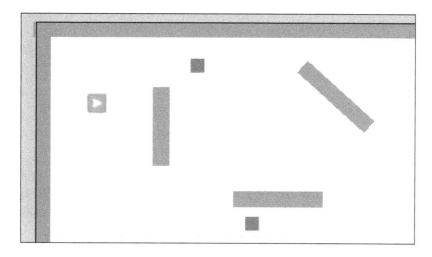

If you test the game now, you'll see that the tank is trying to evade the civilians as they go to their destination.

Creating enemies

We've finished making our unit, so now let's create the enemy objects. For the enemy objects, we will use the same technique we use when we make our units, that is, adding two objects to a container. For the enemyBase object, we will use the buttonSquare_beige_pressed sprite from the Adventure pack folder, and for the enemyTurret object, we'll use arrowBlue_right from the same folder.

After we add them to the layout, we will place them together in a container. Follow the same process as with the player's tank, but with the enemy tank objects. We'll also add the Pin behavior to enemyTurret, and then like tankTurret, we'll pin it to enemyBase when it is created:

Put these two objects a bit away from the player's tank unit, somewhere out of the game window but still inside the layout, because they will to move and search for the player later. Don't forget to put them on top of each other, as shown in the following screenshot:

We will do one more thing before we have finished making the enemy: enable it to search for the player. How are we going to do this? We'll do this by adding the Pathfinding behavior to the `enemyBase` object. Add this behavior to `enemyBase`, and we're done. We'll keep the **Obstacles** property as **Solid** for the enemy.

Making the turrets shoot

We have a turret for both the player's tank unit and the enemy's unit, but for now, they don't do anything, so let's make it shoot. To "shoot" means that it will have to recognize its target, rotate it, and then shoot at it. Lucky for us, Construct 2 already has a behavior to do all of this: the Turret behavior. So, let's add this to both `tankTurret` and `enemyTurret`.

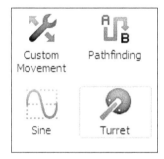

After we add this behavior to both turrets, we need to determine which objects are the targets for the respective turrets. We will do this using the `add object to target` action that will make the turret automatically shoot the assigned object when it's in range. We want `tankTurret` to target the enemy unit, so we will add this object to its target:

We want `enemyTurret` to target the player's unit, so we will add this to its list of targets:

Now, if they come into each other's range, the following events will occur:

- The `tankTurret` object will recognize `enemyTurret` as its target (and the other way around)
- In this situation, the `On target acquired` event will fire, and the turret will rotates to its target
- Once the turret is pointing at the target, the `On shoot` event will trigger at the rate determined by the `rate of fire` property

Remember that the turret object doesn't automatically shoot, but we must create an object with a Bullet behavior to act as the bullet, so let's do this now. Add two more sprite objects with a size of 14 x 14, make them a small circle sprite, and name them `playerBullet` and `enemyBullet`. Place them outside of the layout and give them both the Bullet behavior. We also want to destroy the bullets if they go outside of the layout, so add the `destroy outside` layout to them.

We'll give `playerBullet` a bluish color and `enemyBullet` a reddish color. After that, we need to add the code. Like I explained in the previous bullet points, when the turret thinks it can shoot, it will fire the `On shoot` event. In this event, we will create the player's bullet and shoot it at the same angle as the turret:

Let's do the same thing for the enemy turrets:

With this, the turrets will shoot at their targets. Finally, let's declare when the bullets are destroyed rather than letting them fly endlessly on the game screen. There are two scenarios when the bullets are destroyed: when they hit `tankBase` (for `enemyBullet`) and when they hit `enemyBase` (for `playerBullet`). To add a gameplay element, let's create a health instance variable to `tankBase` and `enemyBase`.

In this example, we'll give an initial value of `10` to the health instance variable of both objects, and we'll decrease it little by little:

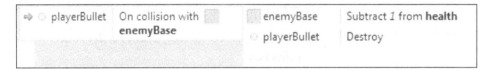

Here, we are writing the code for the bullet collision with `tankBase`:

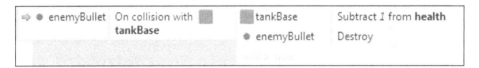

Don't forget to destroy the objects when the health of `tankBase` and `enemyBase` reaches `0`; otherwise, nothing will happen. We want these objects to be destroyed when their health is `0` or less:

Here, we are writing the code for the `tankBase Destroy` event:

Navigating through the level

Now that we have created our own unit and an enemy, let's create a level. We will add a few more friendly and enemy units on the layout, as well as more obstacles. We want to make a level you'd find in a tank-strategy game. You can follow this design or create your own:

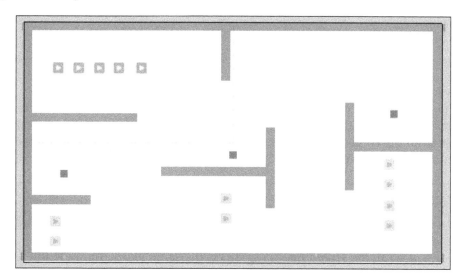

We now have a game in which the layout is bigger than the game window, and we want to be able to navigate around it. Previously, we were able to navigate using the Scroll To behavior that's added to an object, but now, we have more than one unit that the player can control. So we want to navigate around the layout without using the Scroll To behavior. How do we do this?

We'll use the Mouse object to scroll the layout. If the player puts the mouse on the right-hand side of the screen, then the game will scroll to the right; if the player puts the mouse on the left-hand side of the screen, then the game will scroll to the left, and the same applies for up and down. We'll use the Mouse object's expressions, absoluteX and absoluteY, which will give us the x and y coordinates of the mouse on the screen.

This is different from the usual mouse.X or mouse.Y expression that gives us the mouse's x and y coordinates on the layout and is, therefore, affected by scrolling. Both absoluteX and absoluteY expressions aren't affected by scrolling, so they're perfect if you want to know the mouse's position on screen.

So first, we'll scroll to the left when the mouse's position is near the left-hand edge of the screen, the way we know this is if the mouse's *x* position is a small number, for example if it is less than 20 pixels. We'll scroll it in amounts of 500 pixels per second; in this action, we will also use the dt expression; here, dt is short for delta time, which is the time difference between each tick. We will multiply the scroll speed with dt to ensure that the scrolling moves correctly even on slow computers:

Next, we will scroll the screen to the right. To do this, we need to know if the mouse position is 20 pixels from the right-hand side of the screen. Luckily, there's an expression to check the window's width: WindowWidth (pretty clear, right?). 20 pixels from the right-hand side means that 20 pixels are subtracted from the WindowWidth expression:

Then, we will scroll the screen up; doing this is the same like scrolling to the left, but we'll check the absoluteY value instead of absoluteX. We'll also scroll it in the *y* direction to make it move up:

Finally, we'll scroll the screen down. To do this, we also need to know the height of the screen, similar to when you want to scroll to the right. We also have an expression for this, which is WindowHeight:

Test the game now, and you can navigate the layout using your mouse.

Adding music and sound effects

We have a pretty good base for the game, but one thing is still missing: the sound. Construct 2 has an object to handle any kind of sound in the game: the Audio object. This object can play sound effects and background music needed in the game. So, we'll add this object to the game.

Before we use the Audio object to play sounds, we need to import the sound files. If you look at the **Projects** bar, there are two places where sounds can be imported: the `Sounds` folder and the `Music` folder.

The files in the `Sounds` folder will be downloaded before they are played, so it is perfect for short sound files such as sound effects. On the other hand, files in the `Music` folder will be streamed from the server instead of being downloaded to the player's computer. This is suitable for long background music, so the files can be played without the player having to wait for a few minutes for the files to be downloaded. However, the music might buffer while streaming, which can cause a delay.

The sound effects we're using in this example are from the `Sound FX` folder in `freebundle.zip`; the background music is from the `Music` folder of the same bundle. To import the sound effects, we'll right-click on the `Sounds` folder in Construct 2 and select **Import sounds**. After that, a window will open where you can search for the intended files for sound effects. For now, we'll select the one from the `freebundle` folder, which is `SFX1.wav` present at `freebundle\Sound FX`.

After that, you'll see another window that will convert the files to be compatible with browsers. If the icon beside the filename is a green check mark, then it's good.

After you click on the **Import** button, Construct 2 will convert the files to be compatible with common web browsers. The process for this is the same as the one to import music: right-click on the `Music` folder and select the file. In this example, we'll use `MattOglseby-3` and then import it. We now have the required files to add sound effects and background music.

Choosing the right file

There's one thing to keep in mind when importing audio files to Construct 2: file types. Even now, the browser makers still can't agree on one sound format to be supported on their browsers. Internet Explorer and Safari still use the MPEG-4 AAC format (the `.m4a` file), while Firefox, Chrome, and Opera support the free Ogg Vorbis format.

Therefore, to support most browsers available, you have to provide both file types for one audio. However, if you can't, you can simply provide PCM `.wav` files for the audio, as this file type is widely supported, and Construct 2 can convert it to both the MPEG-4 AAC and Ogg Vorbis formats.

 It is advised that you import PCM `.wav` files for audio needs, because Construct 2 can convert them to support all browser platforms.

Playing the sound

Okay, now that you know about the Audio object and how it works, it's time to actually add the sound to our game. There are two places where we want to play the sound effects: when the tanks are shot and when the tanks are destroyed. We'll play the `SFX1` audio file for both events; edit them as follows:

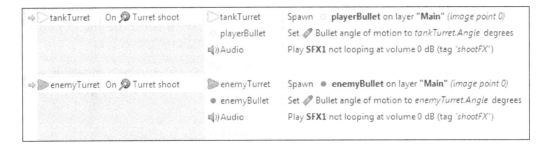

We'll then edit the events where the player's units and enemy tanks are destroyed, to play the explosion sound effect:

Here, we are writing the code for the `tankBase` destroy event:

Now, if you test the game, you can hear the sound effects when the turrets are shot and when the tanks are destroyed, but this game is still a bit quiet. Maybe, we can add music to lighten it up. When playing music, always make sure that you play it on a trigger event, or else you might accidentally start the same music multiple times.

 When playing music, make sure that you don't play it in an event where you might accidentally play the music multiple times. It is a good idea to play it at the start of a layout.

So, we'll play the background music at the start of the level. We'll use `MattOglseby-3` from `freebundle\Music` and import it to our project, like the `SFX1` file (make sure that you imported the `.ogg` file and not the `.m4a` file), and play it at the start of the layout:

Test the game now; can you feel how adding background music makes the game more entertaining and enjoyable?

Making enemies smarter

We created enemy objects in our example game earlier; these enemies are just falling down the screen and shooting, but now we will make cleverer enemies. The topic of AI is a complex one, and it is probably difficult to cover this topic in this chapter. So, instead of covering AI theories, I'll show you techniques that can make your enemies act smarter than usual.

Enabling enemy patrolling

The first thing we want to do to the enemies is to give them the ability to move around the screen, just like our own units. To do this, we'll first add a Timer behavior to the `enemyBase` object so that it can do something repeatedly. We also need to add an instance variable to it to record the state of the enemies; we don't want them to move around patrolling when they're shooting our units. Let's name this instance variable `patrolling` and make it a Boolean; don't forget to change the initial value to `true`.

We want the enemies to go on a patrol every few seconds, but to make it look more realistic, we will randomize the duration when the timer object fires so that the enemy tanks don't move at the same time. We will only trigger this timer once, because the time duration for the next patrolling time is randomized too, and might not be the same as this one:

When the timer fires, `enemyBase` will look for a point on the screen; this location is randomized to make each enemy go to different places. Looking for a random point on the layout means we want a random value between `0` and the layout width for the *x* point and a random value between `0` and the layout height for the *y* point. Thankfully, Construct 2 has expressions for these: `LayoutWidth` and `LayoutHeight`. We can use them to get the value of the layout's width and height:

After this, the enemies will find their patrol location and the path to go there; they just need to traverse it:

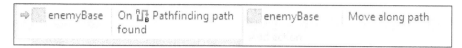

Then, after arriving at the location, the enemy will start patrolling again; we do this the same way we started the patrol at the start of the layout:

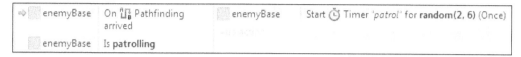

We also need to consider the situation when the enemy encounters the player's unit while it is patrolling. We want the enemy to stop where they found the player's unit and then shoot, instead of shooting while moving. So, we'll stop the enemy unit here, and we'll also change the patrolling instance variable's value to `false`, because it's not patrolling right now:

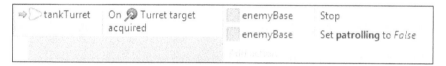

Test the game now and you can see that the enemy units stopped before they shoot.

Creating a scout type of enemy

The enemies can patrol on the game field, but without anyone to guide them, they'll only wander around aimlessly. To make the enemy cleverer, we can create a scout for the enemy; this scout searches for the player and tells all other units when it finds the player.

We'll add a new sprite object to the layout as the scout; for the image, we'll use `red_sliderRight` from `UI elements\Base pack`. Just like we did for `enemyBase`, we'll give a Pathfinding behavior to this object; we'll also add a Turret behavior to this object. This Turret behavior is not to shoot at the player but to recognize the player's units as its target and do something if it finds one. As a result of this, we don't want it to rotate, so let's set the **Rotate** property value to **No**.

Rate of fire	1	
Rotate	**No**	▼
Rotate speed	180	

Now, it's ready to search for the player's units.

The logic for the scout unit is like this: it will wander around at a designated area to look for the player's units; if it finds the player, it will inform all the other units about the player's location so that they can go there.

So, the first thing that we need to do is tell the scout unit to look for the player's tank; this is done by adding the player's unit as its target:

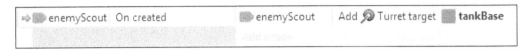

Then, we'll tell the enemyScout object to go to a random point on the layout to look for the player's tank. This is similar to when we want the enemy tanks to wander around, except that we don't want it to search the whole layout. We only want the scouts to search for half of the layout to make it easier and faster for them to look for the player's tanks.

So, we'll add a Timer behavior to the scout, like we did for the other enemy units. And like other enemy units, we'll start the timer to search at the start of layout:

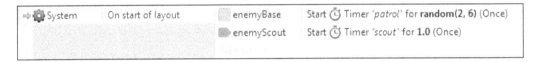

When the timer fires, the scout begins the search. Just like the other enemy units, the scouts will move along the path and start the scout timer again after arriving at the random position it got when the timer started.

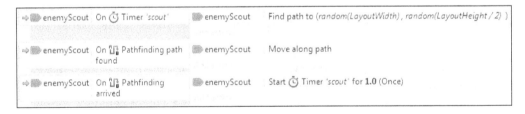

We will now determine what will happen if the scout finds the player's tank. We decided that the scout will inform all the other units about its location, but how do we do this? We can use an array to store the two values; the *x* position will be stored in the index number 0, and index number 1 will be used to store the *y* position. This way, when we want the other enemy units to go, we can tell them to look at the array.

So, let's add a new array to the project and call it `scoutArray`; we'll fill this array when the enemy scout has found the player's unit. Thankfully, there's a trigger that we can use for this kind of situation: the turret object on target acquired. This trigger is fired when the object finds a target in range; this is when we want to store the object's *x* and *y* positions to the array.

Alright, this will store the position we want the other units to go to, but they won't go to this position yet, because there's still no code that tells them to. To make other units go to this position, we only need to add one more action: the `enemyBase` find path to `scoutArray.At(0), scoutArray.At(1)`

This will make the enemy base find a path to where the scout currently is. You can test the game to see how it works, but before that, we want to disable the `enemyBase` object's start timer action at the start of the layout so that the other enemy units don't move until the scout finds the player.

Additional reading

There are a lot of new things that you learned; all of this information can't be contained in a single chapter and still manage to make a game. This is why I will leave you with a list of references for further reading if you want to:

- To know more about Pathfinding, refer to `https://www.scirra.com/manual/154/pathfinding`

- To know more about the Audio object, refer to `https://www.scirra.com/manual/109/audio`

- To know more about importing audio, refer to `https://www.scirra.com/manual/52/import-audio`

Summary

We covered a lot in this chapter. You learned about a container in Construct 2, what its traits are, and how to make it. You also learned about two new behaviors: the Pin behavior to easily follow an object and the Pathfinding behavior to look for a path and move along on it. You also know that the Pathfinding behavior can evade obstacles on the screen, both the default kind of obstacles and the custom ones.

One more behavior that we covered in this chapter is the Turret behavior that can recognize targets and shoot them. You also know about the action to scroll the layout in the game without using a Scroll To behavior. You learned how to import sound files to Construct 2, which file type is good when importing, whether to import them to the Music or Sounds folder, and how to play them in the game with the Audio object. Finally, we used the value stored in an array in the gameplay, instead of simply using it to store the player's high score.

Try to expand this game yourself. What happened at the end of the game? Do you need a game-over screen? Is there a scoring system in place? Can you add your own leaderboard at the end of the game? There are a lot of possibilities!

That's really a lot of things, and we're starting to make a pretty complex game. However, all of the game developers know that all games contain bugs, or at least one. That's why they do a lot of testing and **QA**, or **Quality Assurance**—a process to prevent bugs or defects in the games—before they push their games out the door. Next, we will study about bug testing in Construct 2, and you will know what usually causes bugs.

8

Debugging Your Game

Up until now, you have learned how to make games. You now know how to use Construct 2's interfaces and how to work with them, and you also know how to use the event system to write your code and expressions. Moreover, you know how to use behaviors in objects.

However, we most likely won't write the correct code on the first try. In fact, in all the previous chapters, I corrected the code first before presenting it to you so that you only saw the good code. But now, we will write code a bit differently. I will show you the kind of situations that cause bugs to appear and how to handle them.

In this chapter, you will:

- Learn how to use the debugging function of Construct 2
- Find out what situations usually cause bugs
- Understand more about how Construct 2 picks objects

Bugs and their types

There are actually two kinds of bugs that appear in a game: the **compile time** bug and the **runtime** bug. The compile time bug is the bug that is detected by Construct 2 (or any other programming tools) when the code is being translated into a game or when it is being compiled. On the other hand, the runtime bug is the bug that is not detected when compiled, but comes up while the game is played.

The compile time bug usually appears because there's some code that's not written correctly, or, maybe, we're trying to access a variable that has not been created yet. Usually, there's no compile time bug in Construct 2, because it is designed to be beginner-friendly, and you can't do something impossible such as accessing a variable that doesn't exist.

Solving a runtime bug

Alright, so what usually causes runtime bugs to appear in Construct 2? Bugs appear when we do not write code clear enough for Construct 2 to understand. Let's say you're writing the code that runs at the beginning of the level, and, at that time, you want to show a pop up that says something like **Level 1 begins!**. You want that pop up to show and then disappear at the beginning of a level.

To make something like this, you'd add a Text object to the game and then give it a Fade behavior so that it'll fade over time. Then, you'll add the code to run at the start of the layout to show the text in the middle of the screen. You don't need to do anything to the text after it's created, because the behavior will destroy it. Let's add this Text object to the tank game project from *Chapter 7, Making a Battle Tank Game*, put the text somewhere off the screen, and use the following code to show the text at the start of the layout:

Let's assume that all other gameplay code is completed, and the game can be played. In this case, the players can play right when the layout starts, which also includes the time when `txtDisplayLevel` was still shown on the screen. This is usually not what we want because we want the pop-up text to disappear first, and then, the players can do something to the game.

We can call this a bug because players can do something they shouldn't be able to. To fix this, we need to be sure that players can only interact with the level after the pop up is destroyed. To do this, we need to add a global variable. Let's call it `gameStart` and keep the initial value as zero.

What we want to do is simple; when the pop up is destroyed, we will change the value of the `gameStart` global variable to `1`, and in the gameplay code, we can make it such that the player can't do anything to the game until then:

Can you modify the code so that the game won't play if the `gameStart` value is not `1`? You only need to modify the condition of the events that start the game. When solving a runtime bug, we must closely examine what is wrong, what is not working exactly like we want it to. Then, we'll look at that part of the code and figure out how to make it clearer for Construct 2 to understand.

Picking the right object

The other reason that causes bugs to appear is picking the wrong object in our code. Let me remind you what picking is: it is the process of selecting objects in the event system. If you don't fully understand how picking works, you can write an event that does something to another object, other than the one you want.

Construct 2 picks objects based on the condition of the event; if all the conditions are met, then the actions are executed. Consider the following event from *Chapter 6, Creating a Space-shooter Game* when `playerBullet` collides with an enemy, then the condition is met, and the actions can be run. When running the action, we manipulate two objects: `playerBullet` and the enemy. Construct 2 only picked the instances of these two objects that fulfilled the condition, instead of manipulating all objects.

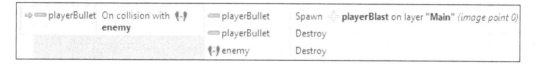

You could pick the wrong object because you tried to do something to an object that's not in the event's conditions; doing so will manipulate all the instances of the object instead of a specific one. For example, if, on the event shown in the preceding screenshot, you tried to destroy a star object, it would destroy all the stars.

Picking in sub-events

Sub-events are events inside another event; the picking process in the sub-events follows after the ones in the event. This means the objects checked in the conditions of the sub-events are the ones that met the event above them. Consider the next event which is from *Chapter 5, Making a Platformer Game*, when the alien hits the floating coin box from below one of the conditions for the event is that the alien should collide with the box coin. The sub-event checks whether or not the instance variable for the box coin is `true`; the box coin checked here is the one that met the condition on the event:

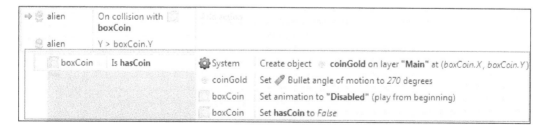

Picking unreferenced objects

One more situation where you'll write the event is where you try to manipulate an object that is not in the event's conditions. One example of this is in *Chapter 5, Making a Platformer Game*, where we want to play the alien's animation. Here, the event's condition only checks for what arrow key is currently being pressed, and the action is playing the walking animation. The only object in the condition of this event is a Keyboard object, not an alien object. In the case where the conditions don't pick an object that's being manipulated by the action, the action will affect all instances of that object.

| Keyboard | **Right arrow** is down | alien | Set animation to "**Walking**" (play from beginning) |
| | | alien | Set **Not mirrored** |

This is one of the places where you should be careful, because if there is more than one alien object instance, then all of them would be affected. To prevent this from happening, you must do one of two things:

- Make sure that there's only one alien instance being played in the layout
- Add a condition to the event so that only one alien instance is picked

You can use unreferenced objects like this when you want to create an event that affects all instances at once; for example, you can create a bomb object that destroys all enemies when activated.

Using Construct 2's debugging tool

Now, we know enough to be careful when writing our code so that we can evade the runtime bug. However, sometimes, there are bugs that we didn't anticipate, no matter how careful we are in writing our code. In times like these, we need to be able to see how Construct 2 runs our game behind the curtains. This is where we need the debugging tool.

While you can use the debugging tool in the free version of Construct 2, some features are only available to the users who have bought the licensed version. I will inform you what these features are when we discuss them.

Using the inspector

You can use the debugging tool primarily by debugging each layout. To do this, just click on the Debug layout button right beside the Run layout button at the top of Construct 2:

Clicking on it will start the game as usual, except that you'll also see the debug tool (called the **Inspector** tab) below the game. On the left-hand side of the debugging tool, you'll see a list of all the objects in your project. The number in the brackets indicates how many instances of that object exist on the layout; the ones with 0 instance means that they're not created yet. On the right-hand side, you can see the properties of the object that was selected on the left-hand side.

If you try to run the debug tool on your game from *Chapter 6, Creating a Space-shooter Game*, you'll get an **Inspector** tab, like the one shown in the following screenshot:

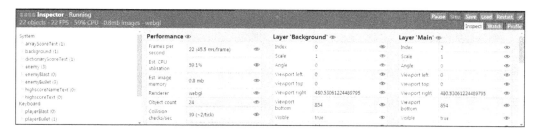

It might look confusing at first, but don't worry, because I'll guide you in how to use the debugging tool. If you click on an object in the objects list, the list will automatically expand and show the list of instances of this object, by their order of creation. The first instance created will be listed as 0, the second one as 1, and so on. Clicking on the index number will show the properties specific to that instance, such as their position and instance variables, if it has any.

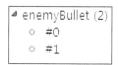

However, it would be hard to inspect the inspector while the game is running, because the value of properties you're looking at might change, or the game can end because an enemy killed the player.

This is why the inspector has the button to pause/resume the game in the top-right corner. The **Restart** button is used to restart the layout, just in case you want to go back from the start to check on something. The **Save** button creates a temporary save file that you can load using the **Load** button; this is useful if you want to repeat a part of the gameplay, but not from the beginning of the game.

Try to run the debugger with our other previous games and see the changes in each object's properties. You can also check the changes in the value of global variables, which you can use to check whether the value of a global variable you write on a Text object is correct or not.

Besides only viewing the properties' values, we can also edit them from the inspector. Not all values can be changed, only the ones with the white background. The gray ones are read only and can't be changed. This is a good feature if you want to experiment.

 Remember that you can't change the property value if you're using the free edition of Construct 2.

As you can see, we can check so many properties of all the objects in the layout; while it is good as you only want to check a property of one object, it can be troublesome to select different objects if you want to check their properties. Fortunately, you can "watch" selected properties easily using the **Watch** tab.

Watching the properties values

To use the **Watch** tab, you must first select which properties you want to look at. You can do this by clicking on the eye icon beside each property.

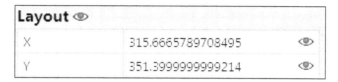

Then, you can look at all the watched properties in the **Watch** tab:

After that, you can see all the properties you've watched, categorized by which object contains the property. When the game is resumed, you can see the changes in these values happen in real time; this is a good way to examine if you think that more than one property's value need to be checked. You can delete a property from the **Watch** tab by clicking on the cross icon in the right-hand side of the property.

 Note that even though the debug tool and the **Inspector** tab can be used with the free edition of Construct 2, the **Watch** tab can't. This is a feature available in the personal and business version.

Profiling the CPU

The third tab on the debugging tool is the **Profile** tab; it gives a more detailed explanation of the CPU's performance. The game must be running continuously for the profiler to be able to collect data. It then shows the estimate of how much CPU time is used in each process. The profiler updates the data it shows once every second, and the values shown are for the previous second.

Draw calls	0.9%	
Events	0.6%	
	Event sheet 1	0.6%
Engine	0.5%	
Physics simulation	0%	

 The **Profile** tab is not available in the free edition of Construct 2; it is available in the personal and business editions.

Remember that the CPU usage is only an estimate, and, therefore, the values shown in the profiler are not always accurate. The details shown here are only about the JavaScript-related processes, while the CPU might be working on other tasks, such as audio processing. Also, the profiler doesn't calculate the time it takes for the GPU to render the game to the screen.

Despite its drawback, the profiler can be used to identify the places where it needs to be optimized if there's performance trouble. We will discuss optimization in more detail later.

Reading the profiler

Okay, I think it'd be hard to know what the profiler shows only by looking at the previous screenshot, so I'll tell you how to read the profiler. The profiler is divided into several parts that show where your game process is focusing on. These parts are as follows:

- **Events**: This shows how much time is spent running the logic in the event sheet.

- **Physics simulation**: This shows the time spent running the physics calculation in the game. Since physics can be CPU intensive, it's a good idea to pay attention to this if you use a lot of physics objects.

- **Draw calls**: This shows how long it takes for the CPU to issue render calls; this does not include the time it takes for the GPU to draw graphics. Sometimes, draw calls can take a long time, especially if you have a lot of objects to be rendered to the screen at once.

- **Engine**: This is the time spent doing Construct 2 calculations, not including anything that has already been covered earlier. This means taking care of various objects' behaviors and other engine processes in the background.

Performance summary

In the top left-hand side of the debugging tool, you can see a summary of the game's performance. You can use this to measure how fast your game is running. The values are as follows:

- **The objects count**: This is the total number of objects created: try not to have too many objects because this can reduce performance.

- **The framerate**: This shows how many times per second the game runs; the game should ideally run at 60 fps, but somewhere between 30 and 60 fps is also good.

- **The estimated CPU time**: This shows an estimate of how much CPU time is being used in the game. This is just an estimate and not always accurate. If you see this number going up, this means that the CPU is allocating a lot of its power to executing your game logic. You can try to do things more efficiently by not doing a lot of things at every tick.

- **The estimated image-memory use**: This is an estimate of how much space in memory is used by the images in the game; this only shows the memory used by the loaded images, because images use up the most space in a game. Note that this does not show the memory used by music and sound effects. If this number is high, it means you're using too many large images that might be slowing down the game; switching to smaller images would be a good idea.

- **The renderer**: This tells you what kind of renderer is used by the game. For faster performance, it is advised that you use webgl instead of canvas2d. There is no reason for you to use canvas2d over webgl, but if the device or computer on which the game is running doesn't support webgl, Construct 2 will fall back on canvas2d.

```
≡≡≡≡ Inspector - Running
36 objects - 20 FPS - 62% CPU - 0.8mb images - webgl
```

Using breakpoints

Construct 2 has a debugging tool that traditional programming languages have: breakpoints. Breakpoints are an advanced feature that can greatly help in debugging your game. Breakpoints pause the running of the game right before the event marked with it is executed, and they allow you to carefully inspect the game objects' properties before continuing.

 Breakpoints aren't available in Construct 2's free edition.

To use a breakpoint, you need to right-click on an event, on a condition in an event, or on an action you want to examine. A pop up will show and select the **Toggle breakpoint** option. You can also erase a breakpoint that was applied earlier in the manner specified in the following screenshot:

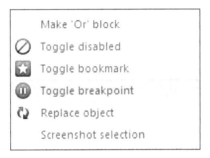

You can apply breakpoints on any event or actions except:

- On triggers
- On sub-events of triggers
- On loops

You can still apply it on any sub-events that are not under a trigger. When you apply a breakpoint to an event, the breakpoint symbol is shown right beside it:

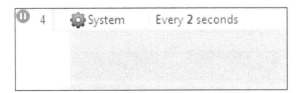

The breakpoints won't work if you just run the layout normally; they will only work if you debug the layout. I did say that breakpoints pause the game before the event marked with it is run; in the case of events, this means that the game is paused before the conditions are evaluated. This means that the debugger doesn't know whether or not the conditions are met and the event is run; you must resume execution to be able to know.

When the debugger encounters a breakpoint, the **Pause** and **Step** buttons change to **Continue** and **Next**. The **Continue** button makes the game run again until it comes across another breakpoint, while the **Next** button advances the execution one step at a time to the next event, condition, or action. This can be really useful when you want to examine the changes that take place in the **Inspector** tab step by step.

When the game is paused on encountering a breakpoint, the corresponding event will be outlined in a red dotted square to indicate that it is the breakpoint that is tested.

If you apply breakpoints on an event's condition, then the game will pause before the event is checked, and Construct 2 won't know whether or not the condition is met. If you have an event with more than one condition and you put a breakpoint in the second condition, it will be evaluated after the first condition is checked. If the first condition is not met, the breakpoint in the second condition won't be checked, and Construct 2 will just continue to the next event.

If you put a breakpoint on an action, the game will pause after the event is evaluated, and all conditions are met before the first action is executed. Placing a breakpoint on the first action in an event is a good thing, because it ensures that all the conditions are met before pausing the game on a breakpoint.

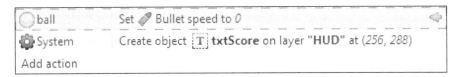

The last place you can apply breakpoints is in the sub-events. Similar to when breakpoints are applied to actions, putting breakpoints in sub-events only pauses the game after the event is evaluated and all the conditions are met. If the conditions aren't met, Construct 2 will continue on to the next event.

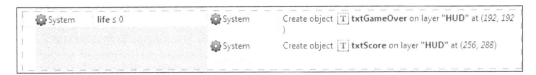

Different levels of bug importance

Before I wrap up this chapter, it is a good idea to discuss the levels of bug importance. Most game developers use this to categorize the bugs they encounter in their games and use this as a basis for which bugs to take care of first. These levels, ordered from most important to least, are as follows:

- **Critical bugs**: These are bugs that make the game freeze or crash or else make it impossible for the player to continue the game. These bugs can prevent the next level from loading or prevent the **Play** button on the title screen from working.

- **Major bugs**: These are bugs that make it very difficult for the player to play the game. These can come in the form of the character that randomly stops attacking, a certain ability that doesn't work, or an enemy that doesn't die when its HP (Health Points) reaches zero.

- **Minor bugs**: These are bugs that don't cause any trouble in the gaming experience but are still very noticeable. These bugs can include the wrong graphic showing up or some dumb AI.

It is always important to fix bugs, starting from critical bugs first to minor ones. Not only that, fixing critical bugs makes game testing easier, but if you're working on a tight deadline for a game company, you want to make the bugs that hinder the game-playing experience disappear first.

Summary

You learned some important skills in this chapter. You know how picking works in Construct 2. You learned about the kinds of events that might cause a bug, and you also learned how to evade it. You also know in detail about the Construct 2 debugging tool and how to use it, including the more advanced breakpoints feature.

Knowing how to debug your game is really useful, but wouldn't it be better if we can write good code from the beginning? In the next chapter, we'll learn the best practices in Construct 2, whether that's about evading bugs or improving the performance of your game.

Mastering the Best Practices

Congratulations! By now, you already have more than enough skill to create games in Construct 2. Not only that, but you also know how to look for bugs in your game and eliminate them. However, there's one more important thing you need to know: best practices. You should know this because rather than trying to kill bugs later, it'd be much better if you can prevent them from appearing in your games in the first place.

In this chapter, we will cover the following topics:

- The recommended file formats to use for assets
- Common things that are recommended for any projects
- Optimizing memory usage in your games

Applying common best practices

As per my experience, I've divided best practices into two big groups:

- **Common best practices**: These are the ones you apply on all your projects, no matter how big or small. Not applying them usually won't give a performance hit to your game but can still slow down your project's development.

- **Technical best practices**: These are the ones that give a performance boost to your games. These are usually used on big games that require heavy resources or mobile games where there might be technical constraints. Though these kinds of best practices can also be applied to smaller projects, there's little point in optimizing a game that doesn't need to be optimized. Nevertheless, it's still a good practice.

Backing up data regularly

One really important thing to keep in mind is this: your computers might crash when you're working on your project, thus resulting in lost projects. Other things such as flood, fire, or someone stealing your computer can also cause you to lose your data. You must always have a backup file stored somewhere other than on your PC, just in case something unexpected happens.

Construct 2 has two features to do this automatically, and it can save data to either your computer or to Dropbox. These features are called auto-backup and scheduled backup, and both of them can be set in the **Preferences** dialog. Setting up these back-up features in Construct 2 is easy, as shown in the following two steps:

1. To go to the **Preferences** dialog, click on the **File** menu and then select the **Preferences** button:

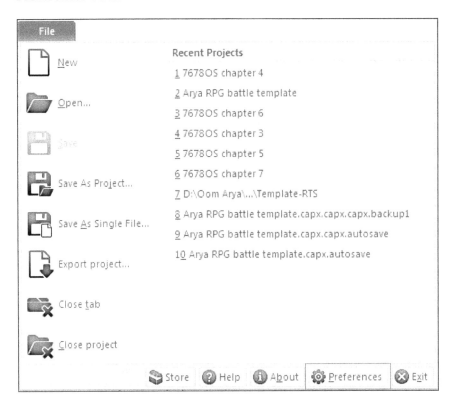

2. A new window will appear. Select the **Backup** tab to see the setting for the backup features:

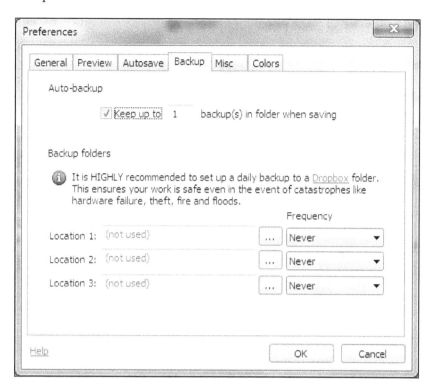

By default, Construct 2 makes one file for backup when saving; this backup is saved in the same folder as your main `.capx` file and can become useful if the main file is unable to be opened (for whatever reason). The filename for this backup is `filename.capx.backup1`, or if you keep more than one backup, it becomes `filename.capx.backup2, filename.capx.backup3,` and so on.

Auto-backup is useful, but it still saves file to your computer. As I explained, it is highly recommended that you save your file somewhere other than on your computer in case of theft or natural disasters. To do this, Construct 2 has the scheduled backup option, which is the second half of the **Backup** tab. Scheduled backup saves the backup to a specified location at a specified frequency.

It is recommended that you have a Dropbox account, where you'll be guided to install a Dropbox folder on your computer. You can then set the scheduled backup to save your project to this folder, which is then uploaded to Dropbox automatically. The scheduled backup is stored in the folder when you press the **Save** button after the frequency has passed. For example, if you set a daily backup, the scheduled backup would save your game to the folder after a day or more has passed. Alternatively, if you have a portable hard drive or USB flash disk, you can plug this into your computer and set a backup folder there, which is a good alternative if you're not in a place with a reliable Internet connection.

It is advised that you make a daily backup to your Dropbox folder, just in case something unexpected happens. This setup process only takes a few minutes, and you don't need to do anything; everything is done automatically.

Testing your game on multiple browsers

While HTML5 is already a standard, the implementation might vary between modern web browsers. It is a good practice to install a few browsers and test your game on all of them. Additionally, if you're making a mobile game, make sure that you test on as many devices as possible.

Supporting devices with touchscreen

There are more and more people using mobile devices these days, and if you're developing a web-based game, it's best to assume that there are people who are going to play your game on a mobile device. To make a game compatible for both desktop and mobile devices, you need to apply some simple tricks that depend on the complexity of your game.

If you're making a one-button game, the kind of game that can be played by the touch of a button, such as *Canabalt* (you can find this game at `https://play.google.com/store/apps/details?id=fishnoodle.canabalt`), you can use the Touch object and then set the **use mouse input** property to **Yes**; it is **No** by default. This will make your game recognize the player's left mouse click as a touch, while click-and-drag represents the swipe input.

If you're creating a more complex game, you can start by placing the **Start game** button at the start of the game before showing the main menu; don't write something like `click` or `tap` because this can confuse players who don't play in the platform you assumed. Then, using both the Touch and Mouse objects, you can check whether the fired trigger is `On touched object` or `On object clicked` to determine whether the player is on a desktop or a mobile device.

After you know that the players are playing on a mobile device, you can show the onscreen controls. To do this, perform the following steps:

1. First, create a layer on your project that contains all the onscreen controls' HUD. Let's call it the `On-screen controls` layer and set its initial visibility to **Invisible** in the **Properties** bar.

2. Then, you can create a global text variable called `platform`; the value of this variable is set when the player touches or clicks on the game the first time. If it's from the `On touched object` trigger, the value is `mobile`; if the `On object clicked` trigger is fired, it is `desktop`. Using this information, we can add a piece of code when the game plays to show the **On-screen controls** layer if the player is playing on a mobile device:

The players can play your game on both desktop and mobile without them having to do anything.

Using the right file format

When working with Construct 2, you might want to prepare your asset files to be in the best format for Construct 2. There are two formats that you need to keep in mind: the image format and the audio format. They are described here:

- **Image format**: For this format, use the 32-bit PNG file from your graphic-editor software when possible. The 32-bit PNG is lossless, which means it saves the file in a smaller size without reducing quality, and it supports alpha transparency.

- **Audio files**: For this format, use the 16-bit PCM WAV files. Importing an audio file with this file to Construct 2 will make Construct 2 automatically convert it to AAC and Ogg Vorbis. These are the two audio file formats needed to support all modern browsers.

Security

If your game ever needs to save the players' usernames and passwords, don't ever write it into events! It will be plainly visible in the JavaScript code when exported. If you need to use usernames and passwords, store them in a database and write some backend code to access this database, usually in PHP, and then, call this code from the Construct 2 code.

This topic is outside the scope of this book. If you're interested in online security, there are plenty of tutorials on it. Some of them are available on Scirra's website, for example, `https://www.scirra.com/tutorials/525/simple-login-using-a-mysql-database`.

Using technical best practices

Now that you know all about the usual kinds of best practices that can be applied to all Construct 2 projects, let's move on to the technical kind of best practices. This advice is really useful to improve the performance of your game, and, therefore, it is best suited to be applied to mobile games where the specifications of mobile phones are not as great as desktop computers. Tablets have generally better specs than mobile phones, but when developing your game, it's a good practice to assume that your players won't have a device with as good specs as your device.

Optimizing for mobile platforms

One thing to keep in mind while developing for mobiles is that smartphones aren't as powerful as desktop computers. So, making your game run fast enough should be one of your concerns when you're making a mobile game.

Test your game on mobile phones from the start. A very good way to ensure that your game runs on a decent framerate on a mobile platform is to test it on mobile phones from early on during the development. This can save you from unnecessary surprises later on when exporting your game to a phone. Also, try to get the widest array of smartphones possible, as you won't know what phone your players will end up using to play your games. If you can't get these devices yourself, you can spread an early (alpha) build to testers of your choice or borrow a friend's device.

Here are some ways for you to improve your game's performance on mobile devices:

- **Make sure that you enable WebGL in your project**: On devices that support it, WebGL will greatly improve performance. Always set this to **On** in the project properties. If not supported, Construct 2 will fall back to canvas2D.

- **Avoid using too many objects**: Showing too many objects on the screen at once can slow your game's speed, so always keep in mind a limit of the number of objects you use. If you want to use repeated sprites for backgrounds or other things, you can use the Tiled Background object, because it is counted as one object.

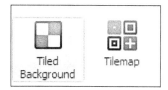

 A good rule of thumb when using images is don't exceed 200 MB of memory usage; even going over 100 MB will probably rule out devices with less than 1 GB of RAM. For desktops, don't exceed 400 MB of memory use.

- **Place objects using the same effects on the same layer**: If you're using a lot of objects with the same effect in your game, it would be better to just create them on a layer with that effect. This is because applying an effect to a lot of objects is heavier than just making an effect run on a layer. To add an effect to an object or layer, we just need to edit it in their **Properties** bar.

- **Try not to use objects with a lot of transparent area**: Contrary to what most people think, transparent areas in your image still take up memory. This means that the game will still try to render them if they are on screen (yes, the idea of rendering a transparent area doesn't really make sense, but that's what happens). If you want to create a game border or something like that, it is better to draw four separate images and create four different objects for them.

- **Avoid large overlaps between two objects**: Construct 2 draws objects from back to front, meaning if there are a lot of overlapping areas between two objects, then the overlapped objects would have pixels drawn on top of them again and again. This is a kind of waste of memory resources, because the overlapped areas are not visible to the player, so try to avoid this kind of a situation.

Knowing the cause of poor performance

Besides keeping in mind about maintaining good performance on mobile platforms, you also need to know what generally causes your game to run slowly. The things I'm going to list are common and might cause poor performance on any project. When your game runs slowly on all the tested platforms, check whether or not you did any of these:

- **Changing text objects at every tick**: Changing text objects at every tick, whether it changes their size or text, costs quite a lot of performance hit. Usually, text rendering is very fast, but when changed, the object must redraw the text and change the cached texture, which can be expensive.

- **Using too many physics objects**: Physics objects are really CPU-heavy operations; using too many of them can cause a big slowdown of your game. Try to keep a few big physics objects rather than many small ones in your games.

- **Creating too many objects**: Even though creating an object isn't a heavy operation, creating a lot of objects at the same time will slow your game down. Always try to design your game to use few objects. Similarly, creating objects that scroll off the screen and then forgetting to delete them will slow things down.

- **Using too many effects**: Just like developing a mobile game, using an effect on too many objects/instances is a heavy operation on most projects. It's better to have a layer specifically used for objects with the same effect; this will make it faster to implement the effect, because Construct 2 can do it in one operation instead of doing it repeatedly for different instances.

- **Using too many sprites**: Just like creating too many objects, using too many sprites can cause a performance hit on your games. An example of how this might happen is when you use a lot of sprites to create a background; instead of using a lot of sprites, it is more efficient to use a Tiled Background object. If making a background is not the reason for using a lot of sprites, this means that you need to design your game more carefully to use fewer sprites.

Listing the common optimization misconceptions

You now know about things that can make your game run poorly, but other than this, there are things that most people think will affect the performance badly, but actually have little effect at all. Knowing these things is almost as important as knowing the real cause for bad performance, since you can save yourself from wasting time trying to optimize when there's no performance gain. Here are some optimization misconceptions:

- **Off-screen objects are still rendered**: Construct 2 is smart enough not to draw objects that are not on screen; the only thing it does is take up space in memory. The **GPU (Graphical Processing Unit)** also doesn't render images that are out of the screen, even if they are part of a single sprite.

- **Image formats affect runtime performance**: The only thing different image formats affect is the download size; they don't affect runtime performance. It is the same with audio formats.

- **Number of layers or layouts used also gives a performance hit**: The number of layers used doesn't affect performance at all, unless a lot of layers suddenly change their opacity or apply an effect. There'll be no problem using a lot of layers with default settings. The number of layouts used also doesn't have any effect on performance.

- **Know what you're optimizing**: One last thing I want to tell you about putting the best performance in Construct 2 is this: don't optimize what doesn't need to be optimized. Sounds obvious, but actually, it's not really that obvious. A lot of people do needless optimizations because they think it's worth it, when it's not; let me break it down for you.

Zeroing in on a frames per second rate

Perhaps the most important performance indicator in any game is how fast it can render every second; this is indicated by its **frames per second** (**FPS**). Modern computer monitors update at 60 Hz, which means that they will update 60 times a second. Speaking in a game sense, unless your game is highly framerate-dependent, such as racing games, 30 FPS is good enough for your games. If your game already runs at 60 FPS (or higher), there's no need to improve performance. If your game runs slower than 30 FPS, the speed drop will be noticeable to the human eye, so always try to have at least 30 FPS.

Understanding which part of the game to optimize

Generally, games process two things: the logic and the rendering. The logic is obviously where all your game logic is processed, such as running event logics, checking collisions, running physics, and so on. Rendering is simply the process of drawing images on the screen. It is not unusual for a game to spend 10 percent of the time processing the logic and 90 percent on the rendering part.

This means that whenever you want to speed up your game, always try to improve your graphics performance first. This can be done by reducing the number of sprites on the screen, trying to use the Tiled Background object when possible, not using too many effects, and so on.

Previewing over Wi-Fi

Construct 2 has a very useful feature for when you want to test your game on another device; this is called instant preview over Wi-Fi. For example, if you have a desktop computer and an iPad on the same Wi-Fi network, you can test your game on the iPad without exporting it first.

To use this feature, we must first enable it from Construct 2. Open the **File** menu and then the **Preferences** dialog. After the **Preferences** dialog opens, select the **Preview** tab and take a look at the **Preview on LAN address** column. By default, it shows **localhost**, which means that you're previewing on your PC. Click on the box right beside the column to show the list of local addresses:

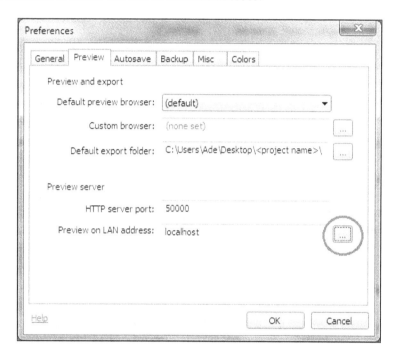

The list of local addresses is the address of your local network; it usually comes in the following format: 129.168.X.Y. Usually, there's only one of it apart from **localhost**; select it and press the **OK** button.

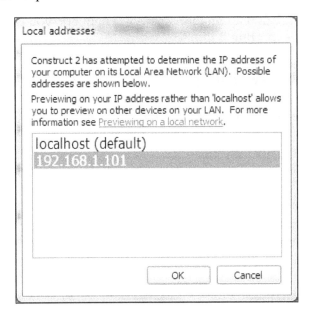

After that, press the **OK** button in the **Preferences** dialog. The next step is to close Construct 2 and restart it with administrator permission. If you run your project now, you'll notice a slight change in the game's address shown in the address bar. This is different for each setting; it should look something like this:

192.168.1.101:50000

If you type the address that is shown here on your smartphone's or tablet's browser, you'll have the game previewing on your mobile device! This is very useful when you're making mobile games, as it saves a lot of time and effort.

 Preview over Wi-Fi is not available in the free version of Construct 2.

Without closing the **Preview** tab (on your browser), try to change something in the project and then run it again. You should see the browser on your PC and device simultaneously refresh, showing the new version of the game. This really eases the development of mobile games.

 For more information on this feature, you can visit the tutorial at
`https://www.scirra.com/tutorials/247/how-to-preview-on-a-local-network/page-1`.

Using your memory wisely

Okay, I have covered the common and technical things you should know when you want to squeeze the best performance out of your games. However, there's another thing you must know when developing your games: memory. Mobile devices have limited memory resources, so always keep memory usage in mind when developing on mobile platforms.

Avoid using large image files

Maybe, you still remember that I said not to use too many sprites in your project, or if you need to use an image repeatedly, then it's better to use a Tiled background object instead, because Construct 2 counts it as one object. Another thing you must keep in mind is you shouldn't use image files that are extremely big or detailed in your game. If you're a designer and want to use an HD image for your level, just know that it won't work, especially on a mobile.

The reason is a bit technical, but let me try to explain. Images are made up of pixels, so an image of 1920 x 1080 pixels will consist of 2073600 pixels. Each pixel takes up 4 bytes in the memory for red, green, blue, and alpha values. To find out the memory space used by this image, we only need to do some simple math: *2073600 x 4 = 8294400* bytes, or about 8 megabytes.

Many mobile devices don't support images whose size is not a power of two, such as 32 x 32, 64 x 64, 128 x 128, and so on. Images that are not the size of a power of two will be placed in a memory block big enough to contain them. In the case of our HD image file, it will be placed in a memory block of size 2048 x 2048; this means our 8 MB file will use 16 MB of memory.

Maybe you're wondering, where's the problem when today's computers have more than 4 GB of memory? Desktop computers often have video memory / VRAM for rendering, and for maximum performance, all images must fit into it. If the system only has 256 MB of VRAM, you can only put 32 of your HD images there, and this is assuming that you have access to all the VRAM. The operating system will use some of the VRAM as well as other applications, so most of the time, you can't use all the VRAM, and don't forget that you'll also use sprites other than the HD images.

This is even more of a concern on mobile devices, since most mobile devices don't have VRAM and use system memory for everything. It is possible that a mobile device has about 100 MB of free memory available. Assuming that your game will use half of the available memory, which is 50 MB, and your HD image uses up 16 MB of memory, you'll only have room for two images. Not so many, huh?

 Images should be designed according to their expected size in the game. Don't just use overly big images and then resize them internally in Construct 2 by dragging the resizing points; this will result in an awkwardly-compressed image.

Doing it the right way

Let me tell you a little secret: no one creates a game level with a lot of big images/sprites, not me and not any other game developer. You can't make a fast game with big backgrounds like that. What you can do, instead, is to use the Tiled Background object to repeatedly use a sprite without a performance hit and use several other sprites to add up the variations. You can also rotate and scale the objects to make your level less repetitive.

The next screenshot is an example of how you can use a lot of smaller sprites to create a level. One advantage of doing it this way is that you can reuse them to make another level without more work from your artist. Another plus point is that you can have your programmer create a custom-level editor specifically for your game, and the designer can use these sprites to create a level, while the programmer and artist are busy with their work; it's a productivity boost!

The following screenshot shows an example of a level that consists of several small objects, with some of these objects circled:

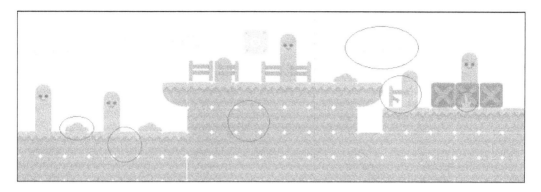

Another good point when crafting your level this way is that you can add this to your gameplay mechanic. Maybe you can push the boxes, or a bomb could blast the cliff; it depends on your creativity.

Construct 2 – texture loading

In Construct 2, textures are loaded per layout, which means that it will load all the textures that a layout will use before starting. This is to make the game run faster, because loading the texture while playing might cause the game to pause a bit. When switching to another layout, Construct 2 will remove all the textures that are not used by the next layout and load the next layout's textures.

This means that the peak memory usage of your game is a result of the layout with the most images, not the total number of images used in the game. This allows you to have a set of sprites for a forest level, another set for a mountain level, and a different set for a lava level.

Mobile limitations

Each pixel on mobile devices can only draw three times per frame while maintaining 60 FPS; this means that you can only use three images of the size of the screen to keep the 60 FPS performance. I mentioned at the beginning of this chapter that an image also includes transparent pixels, so if you have an image that has a lot of transparent part in it, you should consider cropping this image into several smaller parts to avoid getting a performance hit.

The GPU processes an image regardless of its color and alpha values' composition; this means that the transparent parts of an image are also rendered. This is a hardware limitation, and there's nothing Construct 2, or any other framework, can do to avoid this. The solution is to use a lot of smaller images rather than one big image, because rendering a lot of images is easier than drawing a big image in one operation.

Summary

Knowing how to make a game sometimes isn't enough; you also need to know how to make a game the right way. This is to make sure that your game runs fast enough even on slower mobile phones. There are a lot of things you can do to make sure that the performance runs well enough, starting from testing it on mobile phones from the beginning to make sure that you know how your game runs on mobile devices. You can increase performance by not creating a lot of objects on the screen because this slows down the game. You should also remember that physics objects are CPU-intensive, so try not to use too many of them.

In using your assets, you need to remember the best file format to use; use a 32-bit PNG file for images and a 16-bit WAV file for sounds. Construct 2 converts the audio to appropriate file formats to use for all range of browsers. Also, when using images for your games, it's better to use a lot of small images rather than a single big one.

You now know how to make games in Construct 2, and you also know the best practices to use when creating games. There's only one last thing for you to learn: publishing your game, getting your game out there for people to play. You will learn about this in the final chapter.

10
Publishing Your Game

This is it! This is the big moment; it is the time when your game gets its way out of your PC/laptop and into other people's machines, to be played. Construct 2 can export your game to a lot of different platforms, from mobile to desktop to the Web. I'm going to help you to publish it to all these platforms.

In this chapter, you will learn:

- How to export your game to popular web-hosting sites and Dropbox
- How to export your game to the desktop
- How to publish your game to the mobile platform

Exporting to the Web

Alright, the first thing I want to show you is how to upload the game you made to the Web. Uploading your game to the Web means that you're packing your game in an HTML5 game format and want to let other people play it. There are two kinds of websites you can upload your game to:

- **Sites that you control/own**: Sites that you own are those that you have control over; for example, your own site or a file-hosting site where you have an account, such as your Dropbox account.

- **Sites that are owned by publishers**: Sites that are owned by publishers are sites where people go to play games. Some of them allow their users to upload their own game to be played by other people; examples of this are Kongregate and the Scirra Arcade.

Exporting as an HTML5 game

Before we upload our game to any of these sites, let's export our game to the appropriate format, the HTML5 game. In this example, we will export the game we made in *Chapter 6, Creating a Space-shooter Game*, which is the space-shooter game. To do this, perform the following steps:

1. Select the **File** menu in the upper-left corner and then select **Export project**.

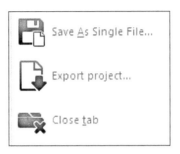

2. After you click on it, you'll see a window with a wide selection of formats to export to; each one is grouped by its platform. For the web platform, you can see that there is an HTML5 format that can be used for most websites, including your own. Also, there are export formats that are customized for some sites, such as the Scirra Arcade and Kongregate.

    Select **HTML5 website** and then click on **Next**. You'll be asked where you want to put the exported game files. By default, this goes to a new folder on the desktop screen, but you can change it to wherever you like.

You can also change the default name for image files and other game files, such as the audio files. You can also choose how Construct 2 compresses the image; better compression means smaller image files but a slower exporting process. If you're not sure which to pick, always choose the recommended option.

3. One important thing to note is that you must always keep the **Minify script** checkbox checked. This is to make it hard for people to decompile your game code. Decompile or decompiling is the act of breaking into other software's code without the permission of the software maker. People who decompile your game can clone it after that. Uncheck this checkbox only if you want to allow people to look into your code. This feature requires Java to be installed on your computer; note that Java is a different technology than JavaScript.

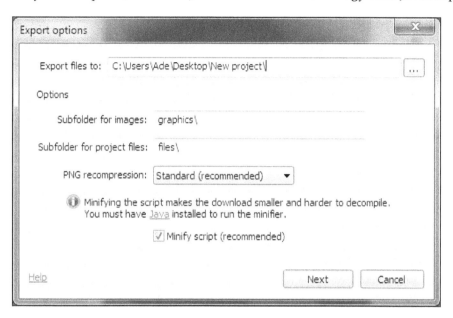

4. After you click on **Next**, you'll be asked to choose a template for the HTML5 game, whether it's **Normal style**, **Advert bar style**, or **Embed style**. A small description is written below the selections to give you an idea of what to choose. If you just want to show your game on your website, then the **Normal style** is good enough:

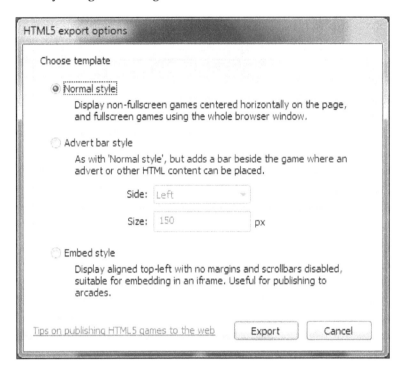

5. After selecting the format in which you want your game to be, click on the **Export** button. After a few seconds or minutes, depending on your game, your project will finish exporting and will be ready to be uploaded to the Web.

 Construct 2 games exported as HTML5 won't work offline, that is, if you just open the index file from your local computer; they must be uploaded somewhere.

Uploading games to your Dropbox

Unfortunately, just exporting your game won't ensure that other people will be able to play it; you need to upload it somewhere. The easiest place to upload it is to Dropbox, because you just need to upload it to the public folder, and everyone can play the game. I assume that you already have a Dropbox account and a Dropbox folder on your computer; if you don't, then you can just go to `https://www.dropbox.com/` to sign up and install a `Dropbox` folder on your PC.

Once installed, open your `Dropbox` folder. In this folder, you can create folders to save your files on the cloud. However, the only folder that other people have access to is the `Public` folder, so we will put our games here.

 As of October 2012, new Dropbox accounts no longer have a `Public` folder. You can enable the `Public` folder by following the steps at `https://www.dropbox.com/en/help/4224`.

Now, perform the following steps:

1. Copy your exported game folder to the `Public` folder. After that, open your game folder and right-click on the HTML index file; this is the file that people will access if they want to play your game.

2. In the menu that appears, select **Copy public link**; this will copy the link we need to play this game on a web browser.

3. After that, just paste the link on your browser and you can start playing.

Requirements for the Scirra Arcade

As the people who made a game-making tool, it'd be strange if Scirra didn't provide a place where people can upload their games for the world to play. Scirra has an arcade site located at `http://www.scirra.com/arcade`, where you can upload your HTML5 games.

There are several limitations for the game to be uploaded there. First, the game size must not be more than 10 MB, and second, the game's width can't be more than 800 pixels. There are also plugins and behavior limitations in the arcade; not all plugins and behaviors are supported by the Scirra Arcade.

To be accepted by the arcade, your game must only use these plugins:

AJAX	Array	Audio
Button	Browser	C2Websocket
Dictionary	Facebook	Function
Gamepad	Geolocation	GooglePlay
IAP	List	Keyboard
Mouse	NinePatch	NodeWebKit
Particles	ProgressBar	ScirraArcade
Shadowlight	Sliderbar	Sprite
Spritefont2	Text	Textbox
TiledBG	Tilemap	Touch
Twitter	UserMedia	Video
WebStorage	Win8	XML

Similarly, with behavior, your game can only use these:

EightDir	Anchor	Bound
Bullet	Car	Custom
Destroy	DragnDrop	Fade
Flash	Jumpthru	LOS
NoSave	Pathfinding	Persist
Physics	Pin	Platform
Rotate	ScrollTo	ShadowCaster
Sin	Solid	Timer
Turret	Wrap	

So, if you try to publish to Scirra's arcade and your game is rejected, check what plugins and behaviors you use. Basically, the plugins that are accepted by the Scirra Arcade are the ones made by Scirra, and not third-party plugins.

Publishing for Scirra's Arcade

Now, we'll export our game to be published on Scirra's Arcade.

1. Just like you did earlier, click on the **File** menu and then on **Export project**. This time, instead of **HTML5 website**, we'll select **Scirra arcade** and then click on the **Next** button.

2. The export options you see here are the same as the ones you see when you export to an HTML5 game, so I'm not going to explain them again. Click on the **Export** button to export your game.

 In order to publish your game on the Scirra game site, you must select the **Scirra arcade** option when exporting. It won't work if you select the **HTML5 website** option.

3. In the folder where you exported the game, there's a game.zip file. This is the file you'll upload to Scirra's Arcade site. To upload it, just go to http://www.scirra.com/arcade/submit and click on the big **Upload game** button.

4. Then, navigate to the folder where game.zip is located and select it.

5. You also need to provide an image of size 280 x 233 to represent your game; also, add a little more detail, such as a description for your game. The image can be made from any image editor you like, and the image must be in that particular size.

That is all; you only need to wait for a moderator to approve your game, and after that, your game is published!

Changing the icons used

You might have noticed that in the exported folder, there are icon files in different sizes, such as 16 x 16, 32 x 32, and so on. These are the default icons that Construct 2 prepared for you every time you started a new project; you can change them before exporting your game. To do this, follow these steps:

1. Take a look at the **Projects** bar and scroll down to the Files folder. You'll see an Icons subfolder inside it; this is where all the icons are stored.

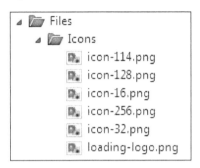

2. Double-click on an image to open the image-editor window where you can change the default icons with the one you have for your game.

3. If you're loading the icon file from an image you made in another type of software, make sure that you properly load the images to the correct dimension size, so an image of size 32 x 32 goes to icon-32.png, an image of size 128 x 128 is loaded to icon-128.png, and so on.

 Make sure that you use the .png format and not other file formats such as .jpg or .bmp.

Publishing to desktop

The second platform that Construct 2 can export your game to is the desktop. In publishing to the desktop, Construct 2 has a very straightforward way of exporting. The easiest way is exporting using the node-webkit; node-webkit is just like a Chrome web browser, but it is designed as standalone software. Being a standalone version, it doesn't have an address bar, a back button, and tabs.

Exporting using node-webkit

An advantage of exporting using node-webkit is that your final game file can be played on all the major desktop operating systems, such as Windows, Mac OS, and Linux. You only need to perform one export process for all three platforms as follows:

1. Publishing using node-webkit is also easy; as usual click, on the **File** menu and then on **Export project**. Scroll down to the bottom, select **node-webkit**, and click on **Next**.

   The export options that you will see next are just the same as when you export to the Web. After deciding where to put the exported files, just click on the **Export** button. Here, you'll see the export options for node-webkit. I will explain these options to you in a nutshell:

   - **Single instance**: If this is checked, you only allow one instance of the game to run; no two games can run alongside each other
   - **Window frame**: Checking this will show the game's border; uncheck it if you want to hide the window frame
   - **Resizable window**: Checking this will allow the player to resize the game window
   - **Kiosk mode**: If you check this, you'll disable the minimize and maximize controls for the window; this is for games that are intended to be played at a kiosk/booth at exhibition places

   These modes can be seen in the following screenshot:

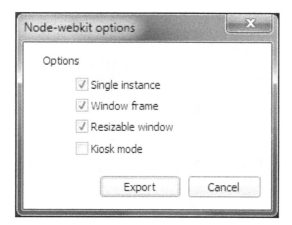

2. You can leave the node-webkit options at the default configurations with the first three options checked, or you can customize something yourself.

3. Clicking on the **Export** button will package the game to the place you specified earlier in the export process. In this exported folder, there are four more folders: linux32, linux64, osx for Macintosh, and win32; each folder contains the game files for their target platforms. The files needed to play the game for each OS are inside the respective folders; for Windows, you only need to double-click on the .exe file.

 You can separate and rename each of these four folders. It's usually a good idea to rename them, so if you want to share the game with someone who only has a Mac, you only need to give them the osx version.

Publishing as an Open Web App

An Open Web App is an HTML5-based app format that any digital application store can use; this format is invented by Mozilla. Even though it is intended to be able to be used by as many application stores as possible, right now, only Mozilla is using it for their Firefox marketplace. Firefox marketplace apps can be installed on the desktop from the Firefox browser or even from Firefox on Android.

As a game exported on a Firefox marketplace can be played on a desktop and mobile, it is advised that you check whether the player plays it from their desktop or phone. You can do this from the tips I gave in *Chapter 9, Mastering the Best Practices*. Exporting to the Firefox marketplace is a good alternative compared to using node-webkit; it is almost as easy, and it's ready to be distributed to a lot of people using Firefox.

1. First, open your project properties; remember that you can do this by clicking on the project's name in the **Projects** bar and fill out the **Name**, **Description**, and **Author** fields. Fill them out with the game's name, game's description, and the developer's name, respectively. This is one of the requirements for the Firefox marketplace.

2. Export your project as usual; but this time, select the Open Web App as the platform to export to. The export options are the same as the ones you see when exporting to any other platforms.

3. After you click on **Next**, the Open Web App options window comes up. There are two kinds of Open Web App games you can make: packaged app and hosted app.

A packaged app is a package that contains all your game files; the player can play it directly on their PC or mobile devices, while a hosted app is like a website but distributed as an app; you'll need your own server hosting for a hosted app.

4. In the lower section of this options window is the **Permissions** section. If your game uses geolocation or the file-storage feature, you need to check either of these checkboxes. This is needed to ask for user permission before enabling these features on the game.

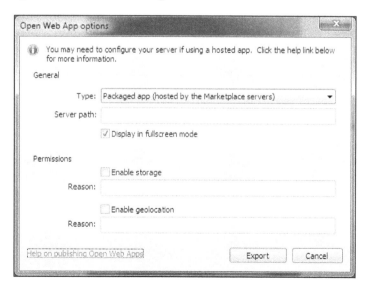

Exporting a packaged app

A packaged app is the easiest way to export to the Firefox marketplace, because you don't need your own hosting. If you don't need any permission from the player, you can just click on the **Export** button. After the exporting is done, go to the `exported files` folder and archive all of them to a ZIP file. This ZIP file is the file you submit to the Firefox marketplace.

To make a ZIP file, first select all the files you want to archive and then right-click on them and select **Add to archive...**:

A dialog window will show up; change the archive format to ZIP and rename it to whatever you want to, but it's better to name it similar to the game you're uploading. When you're done, click on the **OK** button, and the files will be archived.

Make sure that you package all the files in the folder to a ZIP file and not the exported folder where all the files are placed. This is important, as the index.html file must be at the top level in your ZIP file. This is because when submitting to the Firefox marketplace, the marketplace will look for the index.html file at the top level of your ZIP file. If you zip the folder where all the files are located, the marketplace won't find your index.html file, and your game will be rejected.

Exporting a hosted app

Exporting a hosted app is a bit difficult because you must also set up your hosting. Perform these steps to export a hosted app:

1. When you're exporting a hosted app, you must supply the server path. This path is relative to the domain and must be set depending on where your game will be uploaded. So, if your game is located at http://www.yoursite.com/games/gameName/, the server path should be set to /games/gameName/. After that, you can export your game.

2. After you're done, the final files you get will be similar to other HTML5 website files. You only need to upload these files to the Web. If you don't have a web host already, start looking for one that is.

3. You also need to configure your server MIME types; if you don't know what this means, then contact your website support centre. There are a few MIME types to set, such as the following ones:

   ° application/x-web-app-manifest+json: This is for the .webapp file extension. This is a must; the Firefox marketplace won't allow you to submit an app if this is not done right.

   ° text/cache-manifest: This is for .appcache so that offline support works.

   ° audio/ogg: This is for .ogg so that the .ogg audio files can play.

   ° audio/mp4: This is for .m4a so that the .m4a format audio files can play.

> More information on exporting to Open Web App can be found at https://www.scirra.com/tutorials/430/how-to-export-an-open-web-app-for-firefox-marketplace.
>
> Again, if you are not sure about setting MIME types, ask your web host support team; if you want to know more about MIME types yourself, visit https://www.scirra.com/manual/168/mime-types.

Submitting to the Firefox marketplace

Now that all the files are prepared, it's time to submit your game to the Firefox marketplace. To start, go to `https://marketplace.firefox.com/developers/` and sign up for a developer account. After that, you can submit your game through `https://marketplace.firefox.com/developers/submit/`. For a hosted app, you need to provide the full URL to the `.webapp` file, while for the packaged app, you simply need to upload your game's ZIP file.

When submitting, you can also provide more details of your game and select what devices you support. Since Construct 2 is a cross-platform engine, you should be able to support all platforms.

Publishing to mobile platforms

Even though Construct 2 has great support for various mobile platforms, exporting to these platforms won't be easy. You still need to download additional software called development kit from each platform holder and use it to build your mobile game. The easiest way to publish for mobile is, perhaps, to export as an Open Web App and submit the game to the Firefox marketplace, only supporting mobile devices.

 If you want to read a lengthy tutorial on it, there's one on Scirra's website at `https://www.scirra.com/tutorials/74/publishing-and-promoting-your-construct-2-game`.

Another way to export a game for mobile platforms is to use the PhoneGap export option. PhoneGap is a framework that builds your HTML5 game to be ready for the three major platforms: Android, iOS, and Windows Phone. It also has a service called PhoneGap build service that builds our game in their cloud server; we only need to supply the HTML5 files.

Preparing your PhoneGap game

So, just like usual, we'll export our game, but this time, we will choose the **PhoneGap** option for the platform to export to. Just like we did when we published an Open Web App game, we need to fill out the description, ID, and version number in our game's project properties before continuing; after this is done, click on **Next**. The export options here are the same with most target platforms in Construct 2; after you're done, click on the **Next** button.

The next window is the PhoneGap export options; this is where you'll set several things for your game, such as the following options:

- **Supported devices**: This feature sets whether your game is for handsets (smartphones) only, or tablets only, or both (universal option)

- **Permissions**: This feature is used to ask users to allow your game to use some in-game features; these in-game features are:
  - ○ **Geolocation**: This is to find out about the user's location
  - ○ **Camera**: This is to use a camera from the user's device
  - ○ **Vibrate**: This is to make the user's device vibrate
  - ○ **Media**: This is to use microphone input from the user's device

- **Minimum supported OSs**: This sets the lowest version of iOS and Android that is supported by your game. Older mobile OS versions have poor support for PhoneGap apps, so it is advised that you stick to the recommended option.

After you're done, click on the **Export** button to start exporting. If it's finished, you'll have all the files needed to be uploaded to the PhoneGap build service.

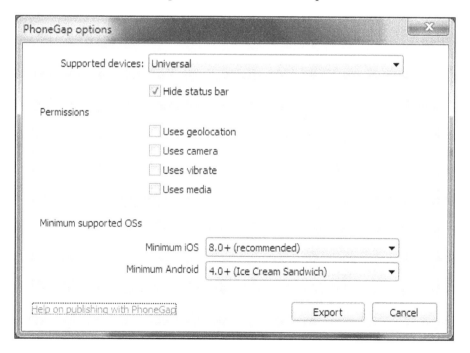

The PhoneGap build service won't export to iOS if you're not an Apple developer. You must be registered as an iOS developer to build iOS games with the PhoneGap build service.

Becoming an Apple developer requires you to pay for $99 a year, and for students, their school has to participate in the Apple University Program. More information on this can be found at `https://www.scirra.com/tutorials/72/how-to-become-an-ios-developer`.

Uploading to PhoneGap

First, open the folder with your exported PhoneGap game files and add them all to a `.zip` file. Just like you did when zipping the Open Web App, you must zip all the files in the folder and not the folder itself. After that, we can go to the PhoneGap site.

To use the PhoneGap build service, you need to go to `https://build.phonegap.com/` and register an account.

After that, you can create a new app; don't forget to select the **Upload a zip file** option. This is where you select the previous `.zip` file and upload it.

You can build one mobile app for free, but you have to pay to use it to build more than one app.

Now, you just need to wait for a few minutes while the site is building your game. After it's done, you can download the files for each platform to your computer. Your game is now ready to be published on various application stores!

There are many more export options available in Construct 2, such as the Chrome web store, Kongregate, Blackberry 10, Tizen, the Amazon Appstore, and the Windows Store. For more information on this, I've provided a link at the beginning of the *Publishing to mobile platforms* section.

Summary

And we're done! In this book, I taught you how to make games using Construct 2, and in this chapter, I taught you how to publish your games out there. Now, you know how to export to the desktop using node-webkit or Open Web App. You can also publish to mobile using PhoneGap or, again, Open Web App.

What next? Now is the time to make your awesome game and let the world play it!

Index

event, writing 21, 22
reading 20
variable, creating 23, 24

F

fall behavior
  enabling, in plane 52, 53
file format
  audio files 180
  image format 180
  selecting 180
Firefox marketplace
  submitting to 204
  URL 204
Flappy Bird game
  collide behavior, enabling 52
  creating 43
  designing 42, 43
  fall behavior, enabling 51
  random generation 42
  rotation, terminating 58
  timer behavior 54
  working 41
Flappy Bird game, creating
  layers, adding 43
  Sprite object, adding 45
force 104
for loop
  about 134
  end index 135
  name of the loop 135
  requisites 135
  start index 135
frames per second (FPS) 184
fun factor, game
  about 38
  challenging 38
  entertaining 38

G

game
  arrays, using 126-128
  bug, killing 89
  challenges, creating 28, 29
  defining 27, 28
  ending 84, 85

example 28
exporting, as HTML5 game 192, 194
exporting, to Web 191
flow, drawing 32-34
for Construct 2, examples 32
loop, ending 30, 31
losing, by life 86
losing, by time 85, 86
players, rewarding 29, 30
publishing, to desktop 198
publishing, to mobile platforms 204
score, calculating 87, 88
testing, on multiple browsers 178
uploading, to Dropbox 195
game-design books
  references 40
game-design template 39
game, exporting to Web
  as HTML5 game 192-194
  default icons, changing 198
  Scirra Arcade, publishing for 197
  Scirra Arcade, requirements 196, 197
game flow
  change difficulty node 34
  change game control node 34
  change volume node 34
  drawing 32, 33
  Start node 33
game mechanics
  about 34
  creating 35
  fun factor 38
  main phases 36
  rules, creating 35, 36
game objects
  creating 16, 17
  layers, adding 17, 18
  properties 19
  state, changing 81, 82
  z-order, sorting 18
game performance, on mobile devices
  improving, ways 181, 182
game, publishing to desktop
  about 198
  as Open Web App 200
  hosted app, exporting 203
  node-webkit, used for exporting 199, 200

objects count 169
renderer 169
variable
Boolean value 23
creating 23, 24
Number value 23
Text value 23

W

Web
game, exporting to 191
types 191
WebStorage object
about 131
local storage 131
session storage 131
used, for storing data 131-133

Z

z-order
sorting 18

Thank you for buying
Learning Construct 2

About Packt Publishing

Packt, pronounced 'packed', published its first book, *Mastering phpMyAdmin for Effective MySQL Management*, in April 2004, and subsequently continued to specialize in publishing highly focused books on specific technologies and solutions.

Our books and publications share the experiences of your fellow IT professionals in adapting and customizing today's systems, applications, and frameworks. Our solution-based books give you the knowledge and power to customize the software and technologies you're using to get the job done. Packt books are more specific and less general than the IT books you have seen in the past. Our unique business model allows us to bring you more focused information, giving you more of what you need to know, and less of what you don't.

Packt is a modern yet unique publishing company that focuses on producing quality, cutting-edge books for communities of developers, administrators, and newbies alike. For more information, please visit our website at www.packtpub.com.

About Packt Open Source

In 2010, Packt launched two new brands, Packt Open Source and Packt Enterprise, in order to continue its focus on specialization. This book is part of the Packt Open Source brand, home to books published on software built around open source licenses, and offering information to anybody from advanced developers to budding web designers. The Open Source brand also runs Packt's Open Source Royalty Scheme, by which Packt gives a royalty to each open source project about whose software a book is sold.

Writing for Packt

We welcome all inquiries from people who are interested in authoring. Book proposals should be sent to author@packtpub.com. If your book idea is still at an early stage and you would like to discuss it first before writing a formal book proposal, then please contact us; one of our commissioning editors will get in touch with you.

We're not just looking for published authors; if you have strong technical skills but no writing experience, our experienced editors can help you develop a writing career, or simply get some additional reward for your expertise.

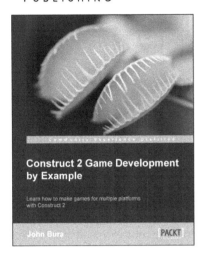

Construct 2 Game Development by Example

ISBN: 978-1-84969-806-1   Paperback: 230 pages

Learn how to make games for multiple platforms with Construct 2

1. Make games easily in Construct 2, with no programming.

2. Get to grips with game design and production from scratch, with no experience necessary.

3. Learn the secrets behind the mechanics of bestselling games, from tower defense to physics puzzles.

GameMaker Game Programming with GML

ISBN: 978-1-78355-944-2   Paperback: 350 pages

Learn GameMaker Language programming concepts and script integration with GameMaker: Studio through hands-on, playable examples

1. Write and utilize scripts to help organize and speed up your game production workflow.

2. Display important user interface components such as score, health, and lives.

3. Play sound effects and music, and create particle effects to add some spice to your projects.

Please check **www.PacktPub.com** for information on our titles

HTML5 Game Development with GameMaker

ISBN: 978-1-84969-410-0   Paperback: 364 pages

Experience a captivating journey that will take you from creating a full-on shoot 'em up to your first social web browser game

1. Build browser-based games and share them with the world.

2. Master the GameMaker Language with easy to follow examples.

3. Every game comes with original art and audio, including additional assets to build upon each lesson.

Learning Stencyl 3.x Game Development: Beginner's Guide

ISBN: 978-1-84969-596-1   Paperback: 336 pages

A fast-paced, hands-on guide for developing a feature-complete video game on almost any desktop computer, without writing a single line of computer code

1. Learn important skills that will enable you to quickly create exciting video games, without the complexity of traditional programming languages.

2. Find out how to maximize potential profits through licencing, paid-sponsorship and in-game advertising.

Please check **www.PacktPub.com** for information on our titles